FROM THE PRAYING CHURCH SERIES

W9-DDJ-856

MY HOUSE SHALL BE CALLED THE HOUSE OF PRAYER

THE 7 PRINCIPLES TO BECOMING A PRAYING CHURCH

BRONDON MATHIS

Cover design by Donald De Jesus

ISBN 9781461109570

Contact info:
Brondon Mathis
614 467-0165, office
816-654-2186, cell
yeshuamovement@gmail.com
www.yeshualifecenter.com
facebook/brondonmathis.com

My House shall be Called the House of Prayer

TABLE OF CONTENTS

PREFACE

Human History is at the precipice of a transition of epic proportions. The earth is being transitioned to the age to come. As a result the Church of Jesus Christ is in the midst of a shift of her own. She's being brought into her end-time and eternal purpose in the earth as a House of Prayer for all nations, in order to facilitate this transition, preparing the earth for the coming of the Lord.

This is the most critical time for the church in all of its history, both in this nation, and in the nations of the world. We must decide what we're going to stand for, what we're going to believe and how we're going to live. There are times when those decisions can be filled with shades of grey and we get by. There are times when those decisions can be delayed or even denied as we live in a time or season of compromise, not being fully committed to God or his principles, and not being totally sold out to the world. But then there are times when if we don't decide what we're going to stand for, what we're going believe and how we're going to live it becomes the difference between our existence as a Church in the earth and our non-existence, our effectiveness as His body in the earth or our ineffectiveness. We're at that point in our world system and in the earth where the church must decide whether she's going to live by the world, or live by the Word.

The Church of Jesus Christ must decide whether or not she's going live in the natural or live in the supernatural realm through the blood of Jesus, by the power of the Holy Ghost. The Church of Jesus Christ must decide whether or not she's going to continue to live dependent on the world system or return to dependency on the system of the kingdom of God. The end is here, and the world we live in is testifying to that fact. Our world is reeling and rocking. Both in this nation and all over the world, both in our economic, political landscapes, and through disasters in the earth seemingly caused by unusual weather patterns, the world we live in is testifying that the end is here. The last few years, we've seen deadly cyclones in Myanmar, deadly earthquakes in China and Japan, deadly hurricanes all over the southern and eastern coasts in the U.S. We've seen our stock market crash three or four times, hitting lows almost three times the low of the record low hit right before the Great Depression in 1929. We've seen our housing market collapse, our Car industry need a governmental bail-out to be sustained, while at the same time we've been at war with fundamentalist Islamic terrorists in Iraq, and Afghanistan sold out to the destruction of the systems of the western world.

The Earth in Travail

Our world is on a downward spiral, fast approaching the end of the age. The Gay marriage agenda in our nation is attempting to rewrite the moral code of the 10 commandments to redefine millenniums of human existence to fit this generation's unbridled lustful passions. The serpentine stranglehold of abortion continues to squeeze the life out of over 1.6 million wombs every year in our nation, wiping out nearly one-third of an entire generation born since 1973. The growing slave trade of pornography, homosexuality, human trafficking, and sexual perversion—not only accepted by the culture, but now shamelessly promoted by it—has claimed countless young men and women, pilfering the Kingdom of the Lord's inheritance. This is the context we find our world in as we approach the coming of the Lord. What's happening in our world? I believe our world is in travail, pregnant with the dawning of a new age. The whole creation is groaning waiting for the manifestation of the sons of God, with these steadily increasing occurrences and shakings in our world being the birth pangs, comparable to a woman's birth pangs that become stronger and longer the closer she gets to the delivery of her child. Our world is at the precipice of the birthing of a New World order. The Kingdom of God is coming. The world is being positioned for God's kingdom to come in the earth, as it is in heaven. These scriptures below detail the process of the earth's groan and what the Church's response should be

> *Romans 8:18 says, I reckon the sufferings of this present time are not worthy to be compared with the glory that shall be revealed in us, for the earnest expectation of the creature waits for the manifestation of the sons of God.*

> *Romans 8:22 says, for we know that the whole creation groans and travails in pain together until now, and not only they, but we ourselves also, which have the first fruits of the Spirit, even we ourselves, waiting for the adoption, to wit the redemption of our body.*

> *Isaiah 26:17 says, like as a woman with child, that draws near the time of her delivery, is in pain, and cries out in her pangs, so have we been in thy sight, O LORD. We have been with child, we have been in pain, we have as it were brought forth wind; we have not wrought any deliverance in the earth;*
> *Isaiah 26:19 Thy dead men shall live. Together with my dead body shall they arise, **Awake and sing, ye that dwell in dust; for thy dew is as the dew of herbs, and the earth shall cast out her dead.***

> *Isaiah 26:20 **Come my people, enter thou into thy chambers, and shut the doors about thee**: hide thyself as it were for a little moment, until the indignation be over past. For, behold, the LORD cometh out of his place to punish the inhabitants of the earth for their iniquity: the earth also shall disclose her blood, and shall no more cover her slain.*

The Coming Revival of Prayer in the Church

Through all of these shakings, groanings and stirrings happening in our earth, there's an alarm being sounded, going off in the chambers of the Church, to wake her up for her strategic inflection of Christ's nature and the Church's original purpose as a place of prayer for the nations. We are at a strategic inflection point in the church. A strategic inflection point is the time at which an organization takes to make a decision to change its corporate strategy to pursue a different direction and avoid the risk of decline. The term was coined by Andy Grove of Intel to describe the period of change that affects an organization's competitive position. It also concerns the ability of organizations to recognize and adapt to change factors of major significance.

Our generation is definitely in the midst of change factors of major significance. We are changing so fast as we come to the end of the age that if the last century Church does not recognize its' strategic inflection point and get back to her first century purpose, she will become completely obsolete at a time when the Lord needs her most. At the time when the world is changing the most, the church must be brought into her end-time and eternal purpose in the earth as a House of Prayer for all nations, in order to facilitate this transition of the earth through the birth canal from one age to the next, and the coming of the Lord Jesus Christ and His kingdom.

Before the return of His Son, the Father has determined that the Body of Christ will be described as a *praying Church* and the bowls containing the prayers of the saints will be full—unlike any time in history. The Lord has scheduled a prayer movement that will sweep the entire planet in the generation that the Lord returns.

There will be a unified cry of intercession from the Body of Christ at the end of the age, saying; *Come Lord Jesus, the Spirit and the Bride say COME* - (Isaiah 56:5-8; 61:11-62:1, 6,7; Zech. 8:18-22; 12:10; 1 Chr. 9:33; Lev. 6:12-14; 24:2-4; Rev. 12:10; 1 Thess. 3:10; 1 Tim. 5:5; Rev. 5:8; Ps. 134:1; 135: 1-3). Prayer in the 21st century church is going to be the main thing, the one thing, and the only thing that sustains us at the end of the age.

The Prayers that will Prepare the earth for His Coming

The Spirit of God is in the midst of releasing a special grace upon His church to establish prayer, day and night, in the earth before the return for Christ, to prepare the earth for His return.

> *Isa. 62:6,7 I have set watchmen upon thy walls, O Jerusalem, which shall never hold their peace day nor night: ye that make mention of the Lord, keep not silence, and give him no rest, till he establish and till he make Jerusalem a prayer in the earth.*

The #1 sign of the coming of the Lord is day and night prayer in the nations of the earth (Luke 18:7, 8); preparing the way of the Lord, or preparing Jerusalem and the cities of the earth to host His presence. There are two distinct ways the Church will prepare the way for the coming of the Lord. Firstly, we will prepare the way of the Lord by preparing a people that love His appearing (2Timothy 4:8). As we come closer to the return of the Lord we will see the increase of a divine dissatisfaction in the Church with anything other than an encounter with the glorified Christ. Church as usual, or church that consists only with activity, with either the flesh or with the gifts of the spirit activity, will be spurned and turned away from in the final generation before His return, for the greater glory of an encounter with Jesus Himself. No longer will we settle for just the signs. We will not be satisfied until we get what the signs point to – Jesus.   No longer will it be enough to produce pomp, performance, or even power in our church services.

11

The church of the last generation will have to produce PRESENCE, which will be highlighted by personal and corporate encounters in our midst with the Christ of the lamp stands (Revelation 1). In the last days the pouring out of His spirit will manifest dreams, visions and prophetic encounters with Jesus Christ. (Joel 2:28; Acts 2:17)

The second way the Church will prepare the way of the Lord is by preparing the earth to manifest in earth, what's in heaven around the throne. Jesus is not coming back to the earth for anything less than what's happening in heaven. Jesus' prayer that was taught to His disciples in Matt 6:10 must happen literally in the earth.

> *Thy kingdom come, Thy will be done in earth, as it is in heaven.* Matt 6:10

> *Rev. 5:8 And when he had taken the book, the four beasts and four and twenty elders fell down before the lamb, having every one of them harps, and golden vials full of odours, which are the prayers of saints*

> *9. And they sung a new song, saying, thou art worthy to take the book, and to open the seals thereof: for thou was slain, and hast redeemed us to God by the blood out of every kindred, and tongue, and people, and nation.*

This is what is going on around the throne of God in heaven – *prayer and worship of the lamb of God.* They rest not day or night, crying Holy, Holy, Holy, is the Lord God almighty. This same expression of prayer and worship day and night, happening in the nations of earth, in anticipation of the Lord's return, is what's going to prepare the way, or prepare the atmosphere in the earth for Jesus to come back to the earth. What's going on in Heaven around the throne must be duplicated in the earth, to establish a resting place for the King of the whole earth to return.

The atmosphere of heaven must first come to earth. The Lord promises to act in His sovereignty to "set" watchmen (intercessors) in their place on the wall of intercession to release justice and raise up a wall of protection for His people, through day and night worship and prayer, during the unique dynamics of the coming of the Lord (Isaiah 62:6,7).

These watchmen will engage in worship and intercession night and day, that will take prayer from the back rooms in our churches to the front room. It will make prayer the main thing in the Church of the 21st century. It will take prayer from being an anomaly in our church services to being the monopoly of our church services

From Rock Pile Prayers to Joyous Prayer

Growing up in the church I know how prayer was an anomaly. Rarely did we pray if there was nothing special or dangerous happening. Without knowledge of how to pray most people will not pray. Without understanding the principles that govern prayer many will not pray with any consistency.

In my Apostolic Oneness Church upbringing we didn't know how to pray, and no one knew how to teach anyone how to pray. All they told us was, "Just Pray." We didn't understand prayers' main purpose, nor did we understand the place and purpose of the helper, the Holy Ghost, in coming alongside of us to help us pray.

So because the purpose of the Holy Ghost being our helper in prayer was not known we either didn't pray long, or we prayed what one leader in the body of Christ has called, "Rock Pile Prayers." Rock pile prayers are the type of prayers that you do, that totally saps you of physical and emotional energy and pleasure.

Not only was our prayers not joyous, as Isaiah 56:7 says they should be in His House of Prayer, but our prayers were boring, and dreaded. Everyone dreaded prayer meetings, because we didn't know what we were doing. In this book on Prayer it is my goal to change that in the culture of the end-time Church. I believe prayer can be joyous, desirable and consistent.

This has been my experience in prayer for over 20 years. In this book I will give the reader the 7 principles God revealed to me that not only made me a man of prayer, but that caused me to encounter a Man in prayer – Jesus Christ. It is my hope that through principles of prayer in this book you will encounter God's heart for His Church to be a House of Prayer at the end of the age, and that the Church of this generation will become a Praying Church.

INTRODUCTION

THE 7 (P's) PRINCIPLES TO BECOMING A PRAYING CHURCH

MATT 21:10-16 (1) **P**ROPHETIC (2) **P**URITY (3) **P**UBLISH, (4) **P**RAYER (5) **P**EOPLE (6) **P**OWER (7) **P**RAISE

> *Mat 21:10 And when he was come into Jerusalem, all the city was moved, saying, Who is this? 11. And the multitude said, **This is Jesus the prophet** of Nazareth of Galilee.*
> *12. Jesus went into the temple of God, and **cast out all them that sold and bought in the temple**, and overthrew the tables of the moneychangers, and the seats of them that sold doves, 13. And said unto them, **(It is written), My house shall be called the house of prayer (for all nations)**; but ye have made it a den of thieves.*
> *14 And the blind and the lame came to him in the temple; **and he healed them.** 15. And when the chief priests and scribes saw the wonderful things that he did, and the children crying in the temple, and saying, Hosanna to the Son of David; they were sore displeased, 16. And said unto him, hearest thou what these say? And Jesus says unto them, Yea; have ye never read, Out of the mouth of babes and suckling's **thou hast perfected praise?***

From these verses in Matthew 21:10-18 there are 7 principles, all of them beginning with a *"P"* that will return the end-time church back to her calling as the house of prayer. This book is aimed at exploring these 7 principles for the purpose of restoring prayer as the main priority, back to the church of the 21st century. This will enable her to fulfill her end-time mission in the earth of preparing the way for the coming of the Lord. These seven *"P's"* that will position the church to be returned to her original purpose and mission are:

> (1) PROPHETIC in the house – v.11 *"This is Jesus the Prophet of Nazareth of Galilee."*
> (2) PURITY in the house– v.12 *...and He cast out all them that sold and bought in the temple.*
> (3) PUBLISH it in the house - v.13 *...and he said, "It is written, my house shall be called...."*
> (4) PRAYER in the house– v.13 *"My house shall be called the house of prayer...."*
> (5) PEOPLE in the house– v.13 *"My house shall be called the house of prayer for all nations"*
> (6) POWER in the house– v.14 *...and the blind and the lame came to him in the temple; and he healed them...*
> (7) PRAISE in the house– v.16 *...Out of the mouth of babes and suckling's thou hast perfected praise*

From these 6 verses we are able to see 7 principles to rebuilding the House of prayer. The first principle will begin in Chapter 4 with Jesus the Prophet.

Principle 1: Jesus the Prophet being seen in the coming forth of the true prophetic in His end-time church is the first step in this rebuilding process. When Jesus came into Jerusalem the people said, "Who is this?" And they said *this is Jesus THE PROPHET.* While as believers in Jesus as the Son of God, we understand the divinity of Jesus – *Jesus is God, not just a good man or a prophet, as some Anti-Christ religions purport* - we also recognize the humanity of Jesus as the Son of man. As the Son of man, born of a woman in the earth, Jesus had prophetic interaction with God the father through the power of the Holy Spirit. Understanding and living in the prophetic reality of Christ in the end times will be critical to the church right before Jesus returns. Jesus said, *He that hath an ear to hear let him hear what the spirit is saying to the church.* Hearing from and seeing the glorified Christ is going to be vital to being prepared for the coming of the Lord. Hearing from and seeing the glorified Christ is going to be vital to restoring prayer to its rightful place in the body of Christ. **In order to seek God for ourselves, we must learn to hear from God for Ourselves.** When you can't hear from God for yourself, you don't pray when you need God, you go looking for someone to pray for you, someone you think can get a prayer through. When you can't hear from God for yourself, you don't pray when you need God, you go looking for someone to preach you a sermon or someone to give you a word. But rarely ever will you go seeking a prayer service.

If we are unable to hear from God, or if we are unable to scale the mount of transfiguration and see Him we will become bored and unbelieving in our prayer life. That's where the 21st century church has found herself, praying bored, apathetic prayers with no power and little results. Thusly, prayer has been relegated in our churches to a few old ladies in the back room we call the prayer-band. But it's this prophetic dimension that we will explore in this first step, beginning in Chapter 4, which will bring us to a place of fascination and exhilaration in the presence of God. Paul's prayer for the Ephesians Church will become increasingly necessary for the end-time church to pray, *"That the Father of glory would give unto the saints the spirit of wisdom & revelation in the knowledge of Jesus."*

Principle 2: Purity is the next "P" of this rebuilding process. As *Jesus the Prophet* came to His temple in His first coming and *CLEANSED IT* of the money changers, the religious systems, and racism, the end-time Church also is going to have to be purified of its worldly lust, which has produced corrupt business practices, sexual perversion and religious systems that have empowered racism, classism and clergy, laity separation, discrimination and control in the Church. These practices have been elevated to first place over encountering God in prayer and hearing the word of God. The 21st century church has left her first love. Jesus the Prophet revealing himself in all his glory will be instrumental in the last century church being purified and returning to her first Love. As the glorified Christ revealed himself to John and gave admonitions to the 7 churches of Asia in the book of the Revelation, in Chapter 5 the last century church will be purified to be a bride without spot or wrinkle by the prophetic messages from the Revelation being applied to the Universal Church at the end of the age. *"He that hath an ear to hear....will hear what Christ is saying to His church,* and she will receive the correction necessary to maintain purity and purpose to remain as a candlestick shining bright in a dark world.

Principle 3: Publish *is* the next *"P"* we will explore in Chapter 6 in this rebuilding process. Jesus said, *"IT IS WRITTEN, My House shall be called a house of prayer."* It is important to note that in establishing God's will in the earth Jesus never stepped outside the bounds of what was written in the Word from the Holy Ghost. Jesus said concerning his purpose in the earth, *"Psa. 40:7 then said I, Lo, I come: in the volume of the book it is written of me, to do thy will O God.* Even when battling against the temptations of the devil Jesus always spoke what was written in the Word of God against Satan. This is because Jesus was the Word made flesh and he always did and said what was written in the Word. If we're going to establish God's will in the earth for the church becoming a house of prayer, we're going to have to publish what's been written. Not necessarily what's been shown to us from previous generations. When I speak of the vision being written I'm not just speaking of writing books on what the Word says about prayer, but I'm also speaking of developing your prophetic history. A

18

prophetic history deals with what God has said, or done in your life in the past, that is leading you to what God has purposed and desires to accomplish in your life in the future. The key ingredient in faith to bring to pass God's will is to receive record and understand your prophetic history. Habakkuk 2:2-4 says:

> *And the Lord answered me, and said, write the vision, and make it plain upon tables, that he may run that reads it.*

We must return to what God said about His church in the Word, and prophetically to you and your life and publish what God wants to do which was spoken concerning you and His Church from the foundation of the world. The creation began with a prayer meeting in the garden, and in the end of the age he's going to end it with a prayer meeting. A written vision published concerning the purpose of prayer in the earth and how God has been ordering your life as well as History itself, is necessary for men to return to a lifestyle of prayer in the Church and remain steadfast in the midst of persecution and tribulation over the years.

Jesus came into the earth because of what was written of Him in the volume of the book. The house of prayer will also come forth in the earth because of what's written and spoken in the Word of her. For the will of God for the church to be established it must not just be preached, or taught, it must be published, it must be written for generations to come. In order for his house to return to a house of prayer for all people God is raising up intercessory forerunners, authors, artist, and film makers that will be moved on by the Holy Ghost to establish in the earth God's purposes for His church.

> *2Pe 1:20 Knowing this first, which no prophecy of the scripture is of any private interpretation. 21 For*

> *the prophecy came not in old time by the will of man: but holy men of God spake as they were moved by the Holy Ghost.*

Nothing that God does can ever happen without it first being written. Therefore before Prayer can be restored as the cornerstone of the house of God, God is going to raise up a company of men to publish the prophetic revelation from his Word concerning his house of prayer.

Principle 4:   Prayer is the next "P" we will explore in this rebuilding process.   Jesus said, after he begins cleansing His temple, *"My house shall be called of all nations a HOUSE OF PRAYER, but you have made it a den of thieves*. When the Church is not watching in Prayer she makes her house prey for the thief to come in and steal, kill and destroy. In Chapter 7 we will see how as a result of our culture of prayerlessness over the past century of the church's existence, the thief has stolen our values, our doctrines and our mission. What we have allowed to be stolen from our foundations, walls and gates through our prayerlessness has displaced the church and left her incapable of being ready to be a bride adorned for her husband, and to stand against her adversary during the unique dynamics of the end-times. Therefore, as in John's revelation to the seven churches of Asia, Jesus has somewhat against most of our churches, because we have allowed the thief in to steal, kill, and destroy our effectiveness through our prayerlessness. However, before the Lord returns He is raising up watchmen and intercessors that will watch night and day until he makes his people a praise in the earth. A night and day prayer watch is going to be the key aspect of the church being re-positioned and prepared for the unique dynamics of the end-times and for the Lord's return. In this section we will explore the rebuilding of the tabernacle of David as is recorded in Acts 15:16 concerning the last days.

> *After this I will return, and will build again the tabernacle of David, which is fallen down; and I will build again the ruins thereof, and I will set it up: That the residue of men might seek after the Lord, and all the Gentiles, upon whom my name is called, saith the Lord, who doeth all these things.*

It is during this time, in the midst of darkness, judgment and great tribulation, as the church returns to the house of prayer for all nations that the earth is going to experience a great revival with many turning to the Lord. Isaiah 60:11 says, *Therefore thy gates shall be open continually; they shall not be shut day nor night; that men may bring unto thee the forces of the Gentiles, and that their kings may be brought.*

Principle 5: People are the next "P" in this rebuilding process. Jesus said "*My house shall be called of ALL NATIONS, a house of prayer.*" In Chapters 8-10 we will see that if the church is going to return to her original purpose in the earth it must include all nations, ethnic groups, races or people groups. In November 2011 at the 24hr Call Prayer meeting in Detroit Michigan, during one of the prayer sets there was a time of prayer for the reconciliation of the blacks and whites in our nation. It was a very intense time, as a noted African-American Bishop in Detroit recounted the history of racism in America, with Slavery, share-cropping and Jim Crow laws, and in Detroit, with industrial share cropping with the Ford Motor Company and Henry Ford. To say the least, it was a very intense time relating, and attempting to pray through our issues of race and reconciliation. If we're ever going to reverse the curse of racism in the earth we're going to have to begin, not with the legal system, or by recounting all that has happened to us as African-Americans over the last 400 years of slavery and discrimination, demanding an apology for these atrocities, No! We're going to have to go to the root of racism, and repent for the foundation that enabled a system of racism to exist – *The Church of Jesus Christ*. The Church of Jesus Christ will not become His house of prayer until she deals with her history of racism that began with Jew and Gentile, and embraces and understands the place all nations will fill in the house of the Lord in the last days. Isaiah 2:2 says;

> *"2 And it shall come to pass in the last days, that the mountain of the LORD'S house shall be established in the top of the mountains, and shall be exalted above the hills; **and ALL nations shall flow unto it**. 3 **And MANY people** shall go and say, Come ye, and let us go up to the mountain of the LORD, to the house of the God of Jacob."*

Every ethnicity and people group has a purpose and position to fill in the house of God. Jesus said, in my father's house (the Church) there are many mansions (rooms, offices, gifts, positions). There's room and a place for every people group, every nation and every gift in the body of Christ. When the church embraces all nationalities and their place in the house of prayer there will be the release of pure unprecedented power and blessing like we have not seen in all the history of the church. In this chapter on *All Nations (People)* in His house of Prayer we will go to the root of racism, which is religion, and deal with this issue that resurfaced at the Call Prayer meeting in Detroit, which has been underneath the surface of our society for several decades now, waiting to explode again at the end of the age.

Principle 6: Power like has not been seen in the church in its 2000 year history is coming to the end time House of Prayer in Chapter 11 as God's house embraces it's call to Jesus, and His mission to and for *all nations*. *Power* in the house of God can only be seen where there is a *Prophetic* dimension, that flows out of *Purity* of actions and motives, with a clear purpose that is *Published,* to empower our *Prayer* meetings, to lead us to the unity of all

People groups in the house of God. When Jesus went into the temple and cleansed out the money changers and religious systems, **they brought to him** *the lame and the blind and HE HEALED THEM there.* Power is always the natural result of bringing the world to an encounter with the glorified Christ. This end-time church is going to present to the world an encounter with the glorified Christ bringing them to Him, not a man, causing her to walk in a level of power beyond anything seen in Church history, where no disease known to man will be able to stand in the presence of the people of God.

Principle 7: Praise is the natural result of a Church that has been positioned by the *Prophetic, Purity, Publish, Prayer, People and Power.* In Chapter 12 we will see how God will raise up his church to be a praise in the earth, and all men will glorify and praise the King of Kings and the Lord of Lords. In the last days the Praying Church will also be known as a house of Praise, a House of Worship. True encounter prayer always leads to awe, to intimate worship and High Praise, and awe, intimate worship and high praises always leads to the execution of the purposes and judgments of God for the earth. One of the weapons in the end times that will be utilized by the Praying Church against the enemies of God will be the weapons of Praise & Worship. Psalm 149:6 Says;

> *Let the high praises of God be in their mouth, and a two edged sword in their hand; 7 To execute vengeance upon the heathen, and punishments upon the people; 8 To bind their kings with chains, and their nobles with fetters of iron; 9 To execute upon them the judgment written: this honor have all his saints. Praise ye the LORD.*

In the remaining chapters of this book we will delve into all seven principles to rebuilding God's house to become the House of

Prayer for all nations from Matthew 21:10-16. From these we will derive principles that will position the Church of Jesus Christ to be the new wineskins to hold the new wine of the 21st century, and be prepared for unique dynamics of the end-times and the coming *Great and Terrible day of the Lord.*

CHAPTER 1

TURNING FROM OUR WICKED AND RELIGIOUS WAYS

> *II Chronicles 7:14 says, "If my people which are called by my name will humble themselves and pray and seek my face and turn from their wicked ways, then will I hear from heaven and will forgive their sins and heal their land.*

This verse in 2nd Chronicles makes it clear that the answer to the problems of this nation or world will not be found beginning with the church preaching to the world to turn from their sins, but in the church, the body of believers in Christ being compelled to turn from their own wicked, sinful and religious ways. This verse is God speaking to his people saying, during times of drought, disaster and impending destruction; *IF MY PEOPLE* would humble themselves, pray and seek my face and turn from their wicked ways I would hear from heaven, forgive their sins and heal their land. For a land to be healed, God's people must first repent. We must start with the sins of our hearts before we can go on to the sins of the world. However, what he challenges them to repent of is what's most interesting. What do God's people in the church need to repent of? Is it sexual sins? Is it drunkenness? What is it that the church needs to repent for? Is it idolatry? Is it covetousness? We definitely need to repent of all of that in the modern Church, but this is not what God is speaking of when he tells them to turn from their wicked ways.

WHAT ARE THE CHURCH'S WICKED WAYS

II Chronicles 7:14 declares that we are to turn from our wicked ways. But what are the wicked ways he's referring to? The wicked ways of His people are the reason that the Lord shuts up heaven that there's no blessing, but cursing, no healing but sickness. But what are the wicked ways of His people? What God calls wicked is far from what we think of when we think of wickedness. When we think of wickedness we think of sexual immorality, debauchery, licentiousness and all types of lasciviousness. However, when God tells us to turn from our wickedness he's not speaking of lifestyle habits as much as he is speaking of our backsliding from our spiritual disciplines in seeking him. He's speaking of the breaking of the covenants we made with God to give Him access into the earth he gave us. God's people are the ones who give God access into the earth, because the earth has been given to the children of men (Psalm 115:16). When we stop looking to him, inviting him into our situations in the earth we cause the earth to be absent of its' source of blessing, healing, and prosperity.

God calls wicked, a people that call themselves by the name of God but have become prideful, acting and living as if they can do what God has called them to do and be what God has called them to be in the earth without God, without prayer. God, in 2nd Chronicles 7:14 calls wickedness a people that call themselves by the name of God, but they do not pray. He calls wickedness a people that are called by the name of God but will not seek His face. His remedy for a land that needs healing is for His people to turn from their wicked ways and REPENT of their PRIDE, PRAYERLESSNESS, and UNWILLINGNESS TO SEEK HIS FACE.

The land was created by God to be inhabited by God through his relationship with man whom he made His landlord in the earth. When Adam sinned and locked God out, the earth became filled with sin, rebellion, sickness, disease, Satan and his demons. In order for God to regain access back into the earth again he had to find another man to cut covenant with. Through Abraham God found a man and a people to cut covenant with to get His son into the earth to begin the healing and restoration process of the earth and man. Prayer is that access and key for God's reentry into the earth to heal our land. As Adam's pride locked God out of the earth, Jesus' humility gave God access back into the earth

> *Luk 3:21 Now when all the people were baptized, it came to pass, that Jesus also being baptized, and praying, the heaven was opened, 22 And the Holy Ghost descended in a bodily shape like a dove upon him, and a voice came from heaven, which said, Thou art my beloved Son; in thee I am well pleased.*

Humility and submission to God's will and plan for our lives, families and destinies in the earth are always the key to an open heaven and God's access into the earth. Pride always closes the windows of heaven and shuts God out. Pride is the epitome of man's wickedness. It is the sin of all sins; it is the sin that caused Satan's demise in Ezekiel 28:14

> *You were anointed as a guardian cherub, for so I ordained you. You were on the holy mount of God; you walked among the fiery stones. You were blameless in your ways from the day you were created till wickedness was found in you. Through your widespread trade you were filled with violence, and you sinned. So I drove you in disgrace from the mount of God, and I expelled you, O guardian cherub, from among the fiery stones.*

> *YOUR HEART BECAME PROUD ON ACCOUNT OF YOUR BEAUTY. Ezek. 28:14(NIV)*

It was this same sin of pride that caused Adam & Eve to be put out of the Garden of Eden. As a matter of fact this account in Ezekiel 28 sounds eerily like what happened to our first parents. Adam and Eve, through the sin of pride, were put out of the Garden of Eden, having turned over the title deed of the earth to Satan. They succumbed to the prideful proposition of Satan, to do what God told them to do - *have dominion over all the earth that God created and gave to them* - without God, without having to seek God, without having to wait on God, or look to God. This is the definition of the sin of Pride. This is the sin that began the release into the earth of all the wickedness, depravity, and corruption that is in the earth now- the sin of pride.

The destiny of a people that are called by the name of God, praying and seeking the face of God is a healed, whole, God-centered land that is once again fruitful and prosperous. The remedy for a sick land is a people that turn from their prayerlessness and began once again to seek the face of God. The Church that has failed to fulfill her purpose in the earth as a House of Prayer has allowed into the earth Satan, and the curse of sin, sickness and disease that has caused the earth to be a barren wilderness in need of healing. *Mark 11:17 says, "My House shall be called of all nations a house of prayer, but you have (allowed it) to become a den of thieves."* When the Church fails to fulfill her purpose as a house of prayer we make the atmosphere conducive for Satan, the thief that comes to kill, steal and destroy, to exist and have his way in our midst. We must wake up and repent of our pride, turning from our wickedness, back to our true purpose and mission in the earth, to become a house of prayer.

The Fruit of Pride in the Modern Mega Church Age

The modern church of the 21st century must repent for turning from the Lord and prayer to the arm of the flesh and bringing the world's way of doing business into the church. This is the wickedness we must turn from in the church - Prayerlessness and Pride! We have turned from prayer to our corporate business models and practices that have attempted to turn the church into fortune 500 companies. Don't misunderstand me I'm not saying that the church doesn't have a business side to operating ministry, because it certainly does. Having excellent business practices in the church is very spiritual. It's just when we turn from the word of God and prayer to focus more on the business of running our churches we are turning from the Arm of the Lord which brings salvation, (Isaiah 59:16) to the arm of the flesh.

> *Then the twelve summoned the multitude of the disciples and said, it is not desirable that we should leave the word of God and serve tables. Therefore brethren seek out from among you seven men of Good reputation, full of the Holy Spirit and wisdom, whom we may appoint over this business;* **but we will give ourselves continually to prayer and to the ministry of the word. (Acts 6:3)**

In the modern church we've turned from prayer to television marketing plans. We've turned from prayer to our latest greatest marketing scheme to gather crowds and influence people to give to our ministries so that our ministries can be maintained, and appear successful and prosperous. We've turned from prayer meetings to service planning meetings. We've turned from prayer meetings, to business meetings. We've turned from prayer meetings to partner mailing lists meetings, meeting on how to cater to our high donors.

This has led to our churches having a form of godliness but denying to power thereof. We look like we have power, we act like we have power, and we preach like we have power, but when it's all said and done we have more performance than power. People are not getting up out of wheel chairs in our churches. Limbs are not growing that have been cut off in our churches. Marriages are not being put back together in our churches. The poor in our communities and in our own congregations are not being ministered to, while we send money to Africa as a marketing scheme and manipulative ploy to cause people feel we are something worth giving offerings to. All of this happens in our most prestigious and largest churches in America while our generation is heading fast toward a generation where only 4% will even come to our churches, or pay any attention to either, our side shows, or in many churches our funeral services. All of this is because our wickedness and pride - *Prayerlessness*, have shut the heavens over our churches.

These alternatives to prayer are not evil in and of themselves. They lead, however, to wickedness and corruption, when they take the place of prayer and seeking the face of God. Business models and marketing plans are not evil. However, they can only be productive to the work of the church when they are God's wisdom from the place of prayer. These alternatives become evil when they replace the power and wisdom that can only be released through a corporate prayer and fasting solemn assembly. We must remember that Satan was a master business man. Ezekiel 28:14 says that because of His trafficking (trade & corrupt business practices) he had become prideful, filled with violence, sinful and operating in corrupt wisdom. When we make trade and business practices the order of the day in running our churches we become corrupt in our practices. When we focus on trading a word from God, or a healing, or a touch from God, for an offering we become corrupt in our practices. When we chose having a business, board, or partner meeting over having a prayer meeting in times of emergency and urgency in our churches, we end up like Satan -Prideful. We end up turning to corrupt wisdom to keep our churches running. Ezekiel 28:17 said of Satan, *"Your heart became proud on account of your beauty, and you corrupted your wisdom because of your splendor."*

Because of the great and beautiful edifices that we have built in the 21st century church we have become proud and have corrupted the wisdom of God to keep these beautiful edifices and institutions operating and running. This corrupt wisdom is played out and manifested as we place a premium more on our offering times rather than on our prayer times. When this happens we have become prideful and wicked in the church and we must repent. When we spend more time having meetings trying to figure out how to receive in the next million dollars through our television mailing lists, rather than time spent in prayer meetings praying for the partners on our mailing lists, we have become prideful and wicked in the church and we need to repent. When we spend more time in meetings trying to figure out how to pay our million dollar payroll budget for the month, rather than time spent praying that God supplies all our need according to His riches in glory, we have become prideful and wicked in the church and we need to repent. When we spend more time meeting to organize conferences centered on bringing in the next million dollars to our ministries, rather than praying to feed God's people with knowledge, wisdom and understanding, we have become prideful and wicked in the church and we need to repent. When we spend more time meeting on how to implement the latest church growth, home cell ministries, than we do praying for God to increase us more and more, us and our children, we have become prideful and wicked in the church and we need to repent.

We have exalted and exchanged having all the money we need to accomplish our vision and large numbers of people in churches above having God and the power of God in our midst. We have fallen in love with the crowds while hating the people, and have equated having a lot of money and material appearance of success, over having the success of God being with us in power and demonstration of the Holy Ghost. Hebrews 13:5 says, *Keep your lives from the love of money and be content with what you have because God has said, I will never leave you, I will never forsake you. So we say with confidence, "The Lord is my helper; I will not be afraid.*

Much could be said about how the church has done ministry over the last one hundred years, but suffice it to say, church as usual is passing away, and it must. Many in the church are trying to hold on to old, dying systems that are unable to hold the new wine of this coming new age. Many are failing to continue on unto the fullness of what God has promised us in the last days, simply looking to an escape from these times with an anesthetized brand of ministry from an end-time theology that leaves the church passive and unaware of what she should be preparing to become and do in the earth in the last days. The Old wineskins of how we've done ministry and church in the past centuries are no longer sufficient for these end-time days to lead the church into the fullness of her calling as we approach the unique dynamics at the end of the age. We must Repent and turn from our wicked ways and return to the House of Prayer for all Nations.

CHAPTER 2

REPENTANCE, JESUS AND THE MINISTRY OF PRAYER

> *Act 3:19 Repent ye therefore, and be converted,*
> *that your sins may be blotted out, when the times*
> *of refreshing shall come from the presence of the*
> *Lord; Act 3:20 And he shall send Jesus Christ, which*
> *before was preached unto you:*

To get back to our original purpose as a house of prayer for all nations we've got to get back to Jesus. I believe we have not fulfilled the purpose of Jesus for His church, not just because we don't desire to pray, but because we don't have the power to pray. The power to become what Jesus wants us to become - a house of prayer – is found in us becoming Christ-like. Because we have not made Jesus our goal or mark in the church we have missed His purpose for us as a house of prayer.

Repentance - The Process back to Christ-likeness

The problem in us not pursuing Christ-likeness is not desire as much as it is our faulty understanding of the process to Christ-likeness. In the Church we have preached repentance to miss hell and make it to heaven. Or we have preached repentance from sin only. However, we can see from Acts 3:19, 20 that repentance ultimate aim is Jesus. Repentance is the process back to Christ-likeness.

> *19 **Repent ye therefore, and be converted,** that*
> *your sins may be blotted out, when the times of*
> *refreshing shall come from the presence of the*
> *Lord; 20 **And he shall send Jesus Christ**, which*
> *before was preached unto you:*

With repentance being the process to Christ-likeness repentance becomes a way of life, not just something we do when we commit sins of commission. We don't repent because we've sinned; we repent because we have not yet arrived at Christ likeness. You repent because you are still more like you than you are like him.

To Repent Requires the Word of God

The word *"Repent"* means to re- think, or to have or consider another thought. The word re-pent is a combination of two words. The first word is "Re"- which means to do again. The second word is "Pent"- which means to think, or a thought. You might recognize better the thought process behind the word Re-Pent by another word that the suffix "Pent" is used in – *Penthouse*. The top floor of a high rise building is called the Penthouse. Therefore to repent is to think again your situation, or to come back to life lived on top. It is to turn from one thought to God's higher thought. It means to come back again to life lived with the Spirit of God on top, leading your flesh, not following your carnal desires.

Therefore, you don't necessarily have to have committed an act of sin to repent. You just have to look in the word of God and get a thought from God that's not your thought. When this happens, and you allow the Spirit of God to turn you from your thoughts to God's thoughts you have just repented.

To repent it requires that you look into the Word of God and get God's thoughts about you and your life. It requires that through the Word of God you're able to see something that you're not doing that he said you could do; see something you're not walking in that he said you could walk in. When you see it in the Word and decide to turn from where you are to where he said you would be you begin the process to Christlikeness. When you see God's ways in the Word and decide to turn from what you're

34

doing to what he told you to do, or turn from who and what you're pursuing to who he told you to pursue – *Jesus Christ* – the Spirit of repentance working in you has begun the process to Christ-likeness in you.

When we make becoming like Jesus our goal we will not receive the Holy Ghost religiously, but to become what he called us to become, and to do what he called us to do. The Holy Ghost is so you can become like Jesus. The Holy Ghost causes that word you've received to go from your head to your heart so that you can repent of your thoughts about God and life and turn to God's thoughts about God and life. When you get the word in your heart and it begins to purge and purify your heart, God begins to manifest Jesus through you.

Repentance and Conversion and the Breaking of Generational Curses

> Acts 3:19 *Repent ye and be converted, that your sins may be blotted out, when the times of refreshing shall come from the presence of the Lord......26 to you first, God, having raised up His servant Jesus, sent Him to bless you, in turning away every one of you from your iniquities*

Repentance and Conversion is different than confession and forgiveness. To receive the blessing of Jesus Christ to turn you away from your iniquities you must not just confess your sins to receive forgiveness, you must repent of your sins to be converted. Conversion is what blots out your sins from showing up in your children's children. It deals with the iniquity, causing generational curses to be broken. Forgiveness releases YOU from the penalty of sin, which is death – *Eternal separation from God*. But in order to be turned from your iniquities, your sins must be blotted out. The word blotted out means to be smeared with the anointing until that sin is no longer recognizable as having ever been a part of you. In order for this process to take place we first have to repent, to be converted, not just to be forgiven.

The Biblical Definition of Sin

Another reason for the misunderstanding of the goal and process of repentance comes from the fact that there is a fundamental lack of understanding of the biblical definition of Sin. What is the biblical definition of sin? It is the Greek word that means; *to miss the mark, or not to share in the prize.* In the Church we have focused on sin as an act, and actually sin is a place and a person before it becomes an act. We have thought sin was a verb and actually sin is a noun - (person, place, or thing). Sin is who we became as members of the first man – Adam. Righteousness is who we become as we become members of the body of the last Adam – Jesus Christ. When Adam fell he was removed from His place in Christ and was positioned in the place of Sin. As a result we are all born in sin and shaped in Iniquity (Psalm 51). Sin is a state of falling short of the Glory of God. The scripture says, we've all sinned and come short of the Glory of God (Romans 3:21). What is the Glory of God?

> John 1:14 *and the word was made flesh and dwelt among us, and we beheld His Glory as the glory of the only begotten of the father....*

The Glory of God is Jesus, the word made flesh. If we've all sinned and come short of the glory of God, which is Jesus, sin is the state of not being Christ-like. Anything short of Jesus Christ is missing the mark. The mark we should be striving for is Jesus. When we hit the mark of Jesus we will not struggle with acts of sin, which the bible calls the works of the flesh. Philippians 3:14 says, I press towards to mark of the prize of the high calling of God which is in - CHRIST JESUS.

The destiny of a repentant heart is the heart of God. We have settled in the Church for being like everybody else except Jesus. We have settled for being like our latest, greatest, favorite preacher. We have settled for being like our Bishops. We have even settled for heaven. Heaven is only heaven, because Jesus is there. When we truly repent in the Church 3 things will be begin to take place, culminating in the life of Christ being restored to humanity. We will:

1. Be converted- *to revert, go back, and return again to our original state in Christ*

2. Our sins will be blotted out – Turning from our Iniquities, breaking every generational curse in our lives-

3. That mark you've been aiming for will be smeared with an anointing that will completely destroy it, leaving no other mark but the prize of the mark of the high calling which is in Christ Jesus - *He will send Jesus which was before preached unto you.* (Acts 3:21)

Jesus said I Am the Way

John 14:6 *"I am the Way, the Truth and the Life."*

When we get back to Jesus, Jesus is the way back to our purpose in the Church as a house of prayer. He said in John 14:6, *"I am the way,"* but to what? What was Jesus referring to when he said I am the way? Thomas had just asked, "Show us the father," Jesus first replied by saying when you've seen me you've seen the father. He then replied by saying I am the way to the father. What Jesus was emphasizing to his disciples from this verse is that the way to access the father is found through three simple truths made clear by Jesus' statement, *"I am the Way, the Truth and the Life."*

37

1. Jesus came first to show us the way to access the father through his forerunner ministry of going beyond the veil, tearing down the middle wall of partition, to give us access to a relationship with our heavenly father through Prayer.

2. He secondly came to lead us to the truth of who the father was.

3. And lastly He came to lead us into this way of access through Prayer, as an eternal lifestyle. *"I am the Way, the Truth, **and the Life.**"*

Only the one who has gone ahead of us can show us the way. He came first to make a way for us to return to a relationship with the father, and to access heaven, to bring heaven to earth. I believe we've yet to scratch the surface in the church on what this way is that Jesus came to show us. We've known and stated correctly that Jesus is the way, but because we have known very little about the truth of who Jesus is and all he represents and exemplifies to the believer, we've not been able to adequately articulate or walk out the way or ministry of Jesus Christ. If Jesus is the way, the truth and life, the believer that walks in this way should naturally go forth leading people to a relationship with the father God, with little to no effort, because our encounter with others is preceded by our encounter with Jesus through intercessory prayer. It should be second nature. When we come to the understanding of Jesus Christ and the ministry of the forerunner we will lead people to the way that will prepare the people of the earth for the coming of the kingdom of God, and our eternal identity with him as Kings, and Priests. Concerning his ministry purpose In John 14:1 Jesus said;

> *"Let not your heart be troubled; you believe in God, believe also in me. In My father's house are many mansions; if it were not so, I would have told you. I*

go to prepare a place for you. And if I go and prepare a place for you, I will come again and receive you to myself; that where I am, there you may be also. And where I go you know, and way you know'

Hebrews 6:19-20 "This hope we have as an anchor of the soul, both sure and steadfast, and which enters the Presence behind the veil, where the forerunner has entered for us, even Jesus, having become High Priest forever according to the order of Melchizedek.

This is what Jesus was doing when He went to prepare a place for us; He was operating in this forerunner ministry of a High Priest after the order of Melchizedek. He was going before us to prepare the way for us to follow him. This is what Jesus was speaking of when he told his disciples, "*Where I am, there you may be also,*" and "*Where I go you know and the way you know.*" He was speaking of going behind the veil to open up the way for all humanity to have access to the father as priests, just as he had. He was going before us as a forerunner to make way for us to fulfill our ministry as kings and priests in the earth.

Prepared For the Priesthood

This is the ministry that every believer is being prepared to enter into when they are born-again into the body of Christ.

And he gave some to be apostles, some prophets, some evangelists, and some pastors and teachers, for the equipping of the saints for the work of the ministry, for the edifying of the body of Christ. (Ephesians 4:11, 12)

The five-fold ministry gifts in the body – Apostle, Prophet, Evangelist, Pastor, Teacher – from Ephesians 4:12 is to begin perfecting the believer to enter into the work of their ministry, which the ministry of Intercession, praying, *"Thy kingdom come, thy will be done, on earth as it is in heaven."* Jesus' return marks the beginning of eternal access to the father in the earth through this intercessory priesthood ministry of Jesus Christ after the order of Melchizedek, as heaven comes to earth. It is the ministry of intercession that we are being matured and perfected to enter into by the spirit of God and the ministry gifts in his body. I Peter 2:9 foretells of our eternal calling saying; *"But you are a chosen people," a royal priesthood," a holy nation, a people belonging to God, that we may declare the praises of him who called you out of darkness into his wonderful light.*

Hebrews 4:14 introduces us to our eternal calling and to Jesus Christ as the forerunner to that calling by saying;

> *Therefore, since we have a great high priest who has gone through the heavens, Jesus the Son of God, let us hold firmly to the faith we profess. For we do not have a high priest who is unable to sympathize with our weaknesses, but we have one who has been tempted in every way, just as we are yet without sin. LET US THEN APPROACH THE THRONE OF GRACE WITH CONFIDENCE, SO THAT WE MAY RECEIVE MERCY AND FIND GRACE TO HELP US IN OUR TIME OF NEED.*

Hebrews 5:1 compares the priesthood of the Old Testament to the New Covenant priesthood, introducing us to the order and process of the high priest selection made in the earth under the law, and contrasting it with the Melchizedek Priesthood of Jesus Christ, saying;

> *For every high priest taken from among men is ordained for men in things pertaining to God, that he may offer both gifts and sacrifices for sins: (Heb. 5:1)*

Then it goes on into the high priestly selection of Jesus made in heaven by God under the order of Melchizedek.

> *And no man takes this honor unto himself, but he that is called of God, as was Aaron. So also Christ glorified not himself to be made a high priest; but he that said unto him, Thou art my Son, today have I begotten thee. As he says also in another place, Thou art a priest for ever after the order of Melchizedek. (Heb. 5:4-6)*

Hebrews 5:4-6 tells us that under the selection made by God in heaven that the qualification for those that are called to be high priests under the order of Melchizedek is that you are begotten of God as sons of God. In other words, when we become sons of God, it's for the purpose of our high priestly calling to become intercessors after a new order. When we're born again, begotten of God, we become sons of God in preparation for our ministry in the earth and in eternity. At this point we begin the process of being perfected or matured to fulfill our priestly responsibilities as intercessors. Even as Jesus was chosen by God the father in Hebrews 5:6, saying unto him, Thou are my son, Today, I have begotten thee. And I am your father, and in another place, you are a priest forever in the order of Melchizedek.

Our Primary calling with the Prayer Ministry

What the book of Hebrews is telling us is that when we come to the fullness of the measure of the stature of Christ as sons of God, our primary calling and responsibility in the earth as sons is to be High priests, intercessors, contending for the fullness of heaven and earth being joined together in one.

Hebrews 5:9-13 goes on to tell us that everything we are to receive as believers from the Holy Spirit, and from the five-fold ministry gifts in the church, from the time of our new birth until our positioning to receive our inheritance as sons, is for the purpose of perfecting us and maturing us for this Melchizedek order of our priestly calling.

> *And being made perfect, he became the author of eternal salvation unto all them that obey him; 10 called of God an high priest after the order of Melchizedek. 11 Of whom we have many things to say, and hard to be uttered, seeing ye are dull of hearing. 12 For when the time ye ought to be teachers, ye have need that one teach you again which be the first principles of the oracles of God; and are become such as have need of milk, and not of strong meat. 13 For every one that uses milk is unskillful in the word of righteousness: for he is a babe. (Heb 5:9-13)*

Are we on Milk or Meat in the Church

Hebrews 5:11 says, *there is much to say about this, but it is hard to explain because you are slow to learn*. It goes on to say, that by this time you ought to be teachers, you need someone to teach you the elementary truths of God's word all over again. You need milk, not solid food! That solid food that is being spoken of here is the teaching and truth of the ministry of the Melchizedek priesthood, which all believers are to be prepared to enter into. But he tells them that they are not ready to receive this truth of the calling or enter into the purpose of this calling because they are dull of hearing. In other words, in our modern vernacular the Hebrew writer might had put it to the 21st century church like this; *"There's much to say about this subject of Melchizedek, and I would tell you more but you have become religious. You are too busy having Church to grasp the main purpose of these elementary principles that are supposed to bring you to the point of becoming the church.* Then Hebrews 6 goes on to tell us that we are to leave the elementary teachings about Christ and go on to PERFECTION; *(Remember Eph 4:12, we are being PERFECTED to do the work of the ministry)* The perfection for the work of the ministry is the calling of the saints to the intercessory ministry of the Melchizedek priesthood.

Stuck on the Milk in the Church

The Hebrew writer is saying, Instead of going on to be perfected to do the work of the priesthood ministry of Jesus Christ after the order of Melchizedek they were continuing to hang out around the first principles of the doctrine of Christ. Hebrews 6:1-3 relates to us what the elementary principles of the milk of the doctrine of Christ are.

> *Heb 6:1 Wherefore leaving the doctrine of the first principles of Christ, let us press on unto perfection; not laying again a foundation of repentance from dead works, and of faith toward God, 2 of the teaching of baptisms, and of laying on of hands, and of resurrection of the dead, and of eternal judgment. 3 And this will we do, if God permit.*

These verses are telling us that all of these elementary principles, which are; 1) Repentance 2) Faith 3) Baptisms, 4) laying on of hands, 5) the resurrection of the dead, and 6) eternal judgments, are all for the maturing of the believer to enter into her priesthood ministry of Jesus Christ after the Melchizedek.

This is where 95% of the modern churches have stopped. This is where 95 % of the Church is today, drinking from the milk of the first principles of the doctrine of Christ, as we teach on faith, lay hands on the sick, impart the gifts, preach and teach on baptisms and speak in tongues, even as we are becoming more and more ineffective in our regions, reaching our world with the message of Jesus Christ. We are failing to go on from the milk of having Church on unto the Meat of becoming the Church – A house of Prayer for all Nations.

In other words, all the things in ministry in the church that we receive from the five-fold ministry gifts are perfecting us to be able to pray, to be intercessors, priests of the most-high God, interceding for heaven to come to earth. This is our highest and eternal calling. However, because we see these things we do in church as the end and not the means to the end of preparing us to enter into our priestly ministry, many in the church have become bored, apathetic and empty, frustrated with Church as usual. WHY? Because any time we operate and function in things that were meant to be a means to an end as though they were the end we will soon become religious and/or get burned out with just having Church.

In Danger of a Curse

Furthermore, Hebrews 6:8 even goes so far as to say that if we receive all of these first principles of the Doctrine of Christ without producing the fruit of maturing on unto this ministry of intercession for bringing heaven to earth, our life in Christ is worthless and we are in danger of being cursed, and in the end all our works would be burned up.

> *Heb 6:7 For the land which hath drunk the rain that cometh oft upon it, and brings forth herbs meet for them for whose sake it is also tilled, receives blessing from God: 8 but if it bears thorns and thistles, it is rejected and nigh unto a curse; whose end is to be burned. 9 But, beloved, we are persuaded better things of you, and things that accompany salvation, though we thus speak:*

Hebrews uniquely describes this ministry as a priesthood ministry of intercession, and the way of Jesus Christ for every believer to enter into.   This was Jesus' eternal ministry that he came to prepare us for – *intercession for heaven to come to earth.*

When we truly repent, returning to Jesus and His ministry of intercession unto reconciliation to the Father, we will become a people of prayer and a kingdom of Priests after the order of Melchizedek – *A House of Prayer for all Nations.*

My House shall be Called the House of Prayer

CHAPTER 3

A WORLD WIDE PRAYER MOVEMENT – *THE ANNA CALLING*

> *"Now there was one Anna, a prophetess, the daughter of Phanuel, of the tribe of Asher. She was of great age, and had lived with a husband seven years from her virginity. And this woman was a widow of 84 years who did not depart from the temple, but served God with fasting and prayers night and day. Luke 2:36-38*

Anna is a remarkable figure in the Word of God of what God will do in releasing intercessors to begin to pray for the return of Jesus right before the return of the Lord. What we know of her is that as a young woman she lost her husband of seven years and from that point on, for sixty years, she was found night and day in the temple, serving the Lord in fasting and prayer. She was an intercessor, crying out to God continually, a prophetess, operating in the power of the Holy Spirit, and an evangelist, telling all about Jesus the Redeemer when He was born. Her life serves as a powerful portrait of a specific grace that the Lord will give to many before His Return. Necessary to the First Coming of Jesus was this woman called Anna who served the Lord for some sixty years in prayer and fasting night and day in the temple. *Anna is a picture and a promise of what God will do among a whole company of people before the Return of Christ.*

God demands that this "cry" be in place before He sends His Son. Jesus' Return will not happen *except in response* to the cry of the praying church. Vital to the Church at large becoming a praying Church is the role of those who live like Anna lived, in extravagant abundance of prayer and fasting over many decades.

By their response and their faithfulness, these will raise the water level in the prayer ministry of the Church worldwide—an indispensable role in God's universal plan to send His Son in response to a Church crying "Come!" (Rev. 22:17).

Prophetic promises will only come forth in the context of being birthed through persevering prayer. God longs for partnership with His people on the earth.   He will starve us out of our passivity, our over-busy lifestyles, and our independence until we do it His way.   Intercession is the primary means that God has chosen to release His government both in His relationship with Jesus within the fellowship of the Trinity and with His people now and forever. The mystery of intercession is that we tell God what He tells us to tell Him to release His power.

> [25] *Therefore He is also able to save to the uttermost those who come to God through Him, since He always lives to make intercession for them. (Heb. 7:25)*

> [34] *Christ...at the right hand of God, who makes intercession for us. (Rom. 8:34)*

God is waiting for our persistence in prayer before Him. Isaiah taught that He longs to release His grace and power, but *actually waits until He hears the cry of His people in intercession* (Is. 30:18-19). Prayer in the 21st century church is no longer going to be a side-bar to everything else that goes in the church.   Neither is prayer in the church going to be something we do to obtain something from God, to get a stronger anointing, or to build the biggest and most beautiful church or ministry.

Teach us How to Pray

Prayer in the 21st century church is going to be the main thing, the one thing, and the only thing that sustains us at the end of the age. Growing up in the church I know how prayer was either an anomaly, something we did when we were in trouble, or when something tragic or dangerous was happening. Rarely did we pray if there was nothing special or dangerous happening.

As I said in the introduction, in my Apostolic Oneness Church upbringing we didn't know how to pray, and no one knew how to teach anyone how to pray. All they told us was to do it. "Just Pray." We didn't understand prayers' main purpose, nor did we understand the place and purpose of the helper, the Holy Ghost, in coming alongside of us to help us pray. So because the purpose of the Holy Ghost being our helper in prayer was not known we either didn't pray long, or we prayed what we call at IHOP-KC, "Rock Pile Prayers." Rock pile prayers are the type of prayers that you do, that totally sap you of physical and emotional energy and pleasure. Not only was our prayers not joyous, as Isaiah 56:7 says they are to be in His House of Prayer, but our prayers were boring, and dreaded. Everyone dreaded prayer meetings, because we didn't know what we were doing.

Becoming Addicted to Prayer

I remember the time I got addicted to prayer when I was 23 years old. I had been in a tumultuous dating relationship with a girl that I thought I loved and that I thought I wanted to marry. When the relationship ended, it seemed that my heart was broken into fine little pieces. I was totally devastated. As I lay in bed one night, I remember crying out to God to come and help me. I said, God If you don't take this pain and hurt from my heart, I'm going to end my life right here tonight. When I prayed that prayer I began to cry like a baby.

As I begin crying, the Holy Ghost came upon me and I began to speak in tongues as the spirit gave utterance. This was not a common practice for me.

Even though I had previously received the baptism of the Holy Ghost when I was 11 years old, I had rarely spoken in tongues since that time. The Baptism in the Holy Ghost in our traditional Pentecostal church was not for prayer, but only a badge of honor to say we had something that other Christians didn't. We never understood truly what the Holy Ghost was really for. We just used it as a trophy on our proverbial mantle piece, indicating that we were truly saved by God.

However, this night when I was in need the most, the spirit of the Lord came upon me at 3:00am in the morning, and for 3 hours I was speaking in tongues. As I spoke in tongues it was as if the Lord himself had stepped into my apartment room and had sat on my bed and began to comfort and caress my heart. When I came out of the presence of the Lord I felt light as a feather. I felt as if I could float to the bathroom.

As I came out of the presence of the Lord, the alarm clock in my room was ringing, and it had been ringing for over an hour. I was an hour late getting up for work that morning. I had not over slept, but I had over prayed. However, when I got up to get ready I was feeling the best I had felt in months. I got in the shower, singing and praising God. I was so high in the Holy Ghost I had forgotten what I had been brokenhearted about. I had literally forgotten the girl's name that had hurt me.

My House shall be Called the House of Prayer

When I left for work I was about 15 minutes late, so that morning I went a little faster than I was used to going, and as I did, I was singing and praising God all the way there. When I got to work my boss wanted to know why I was late, as he looked in my eyes, he asked me, *"Have you been Smoking something?" You look like you're high.* I said, no Sir. He said to get to work and you've got to make up for being late.

When I begin working, I made up the difference of being late in no time at all, as I sang, worshipped and worked with a joy in my heart. That was until about 11:45, when I slowly but surely begin to feel the heaviness coming back upon me. I remembered what I had been hurt about, along with her name and her scent. As I did, I realized what I needed. I needed another dose of the Holy Ghost. And with lunch 15 minutes away, I knew what I needed to do. I needed to skip eating and find a place to pray. That day I went throughout the office building I was working in, until I found a little Catholic prayer room, which was used for meditation, reading and reflection. I remember thinking I hope no one is in here because I need more than meditation. I need God to visit me again with the power of the Holy Ghost.

When I walked in the meditation room, no one was in there. I fell to my knees, I said "GOD HELP," and out of my belly began to flow rivers of living water. I began to speak in tongues as the spirit of God gave utterance. I felt the presence of God as I had felt Him at 3:00 am that morning. The Lord began to caress my heart again, and comfort my soul. Before I knew it, an hour had passed. However lunch was only 45 minutes. I was 15 minutes late again getting back from lunch. As I raced back to my work station I remember thinking, *"God, I appreciate your presence comforting me, but you're going to get me fired"* Well, as I came back to the room where we were working, my boss called me over to his desk.

When he saw me, he looked me in my eyes and again thought I was high, and said, *"Are you on drugs."* I said, NO! I'm a Christian I don't do drugs. He said, that's what I thought, but you're on something. I said, I've been praying. He asked, does praying make you look and feel like you're on drugs? He told me to get back to work and not to be late again. As I went back to my desk, I began to work, sing and praise with a joy that superseded the earlier feeling that morning. All afternoon I felt the presence of God on me as I produced a higher quota of work than I had ever produced on my job.

Things were going great and I was feeling great, until about 5:30 that evening, a half hour before I was to get off work. I felt the heaviness come back, thinking about going home alone to my apartment. However, as the heaviness came upon me I knew what I needed. I needed another dose of the Holy Ghost. Soon as I got off work, I ran to my car, jumped in my car and raced home, not able to get my keys out of my pocket fast enough to get in my apartment.

As I entered that apartment, I ran to my room and fell on my knees, crying out, *"God I need another dose of the Holy Ghost."* As I did, He came in again to my bedroom, and baptized me afresh. This went on for the next year and a half, morning, noon, and night, until I was completely addicted to the Holy Ghost. Six months after, the Lord had totally healed my heart, but I was still addicted to His spirit. I needed Him more than I needed my next breath.

The Wine of the Holy Ghost

It was out of this experience that I understood what Ephesians 5:18 was all about.

> *18 And be not drunk with wine, wherein is excess;*
> *but be filled with the Spirit; (Eph 5:18)*

My House shall be Called the House of Prayer

It was a year and a half later and I was now in Bible College. I had been praying morning, noon, and night in the Holy Ghost for all of that time. One day I was in the 8am class and the teacher was getting on the students for being late to the class. He made an announcement, "Tomorrow at 8:01 sharp the doors are going to be closed and locked, and anyone that is not in the class by that time will not be able to get in and be marked absent for the day."

Well, at that point, I made up in my mind that I would skip prayer the next morning to assure that I wasn't late for class for over praying. So the next morning I skipped my time with the Lord, thinking that I was going to a Bible School that opens the day with prayer and the word, and I will get what I need there. When I got there that morning, we didn't have prayer time that day. We went right into the class. As I was listening to the teaching my left arm began shaking on the desk. The student on the left grabbed my arm and asked why I was shaking. She said you're shaking the whole table. Please stop!

Then my right arm started shaking. The student on the right grabbed my arm and said do you know you're shaking? She then said, "Do you take medicine?" Did you forget to take your medicine or something?" I said I don't take medicine, as I folded both arms across my chest. I began shaking violently. I said to myself, "What's happening to me? About that time, the Spirit of God spoke up inside of me, and said, *"You're addicted to the Holy Ghost, and you haven't had your fix this morning."* I said to myself, Brondon, you better get out of here before you go into complete withdraws right here in the class. I got up, ran to my car and drove home to my apartment, and cried out, *"GOD, I NEED ANOTHER DOSE OF THE HOLY GHOST.*

It was in this context that my prayer life was developed, a life of dependency upon the Holy Spirit, a life of prophetic seeing and hearing, a life of faith and power, a life of joy, love and expectancy of God breaking in at any time. From this prayer life of a discipline to pray three times a day in the Holy Ghost for about 10 years, the Spirit of the Lord placed me supernaturally in the nations of the world, from Israel, to Japan, to Africa, to the Caribbean Islands, as well as many other nations of the world, to pray and minister the gospel in partnership with the Spirit of God.

This is the type of partnership that God is going to use all over the world at the end of the age, to birth forth the second coming of the Lord out of the praying church. Not necessarily just like he did for me, in training me in prayer in the Holy Ghost. But however he trains you to pray, He's coming together with His praying church to reveal His plans and purposes for the end times and the coming of His son to be married to His bride.

Anna: Sustained Grace to Enter a Life of Prayer and Fasting

There was a grace before the new covenant to enter into a life of prayer and fasting. The Spirit of God wooed this woman Anna as a picture of a ministry that would be released before the second coming. The whole drama of Luke 1 and 2 is a picture of how God sends His Son unto the earth. The way the unchanging Father sent Him the first time is but a dress rehearsal for how He will send Him the second time. Anna entered into a sustained grace that lasted *60 years*. This was a grace found in the *old covenant*. How much more grace will be given to the generation when the Lord returns with the power of grace in the *new covenant*?

What does sustained grace in the place of prayer and fasting look like? It is about relationship, communion and intimacy with the God-Man. It is standing in the gap between this age and the next with a heart gripped in lovesickness and mourning. It is about taking our position in that gap and crying out to the Father in unity with the Spirit for the Return of His Son. *God is raising up intercessors all across the globe that will love Him by their groan.* We will ache with what He aches with. We will long for what He longs for. We will not be okay to live in a darkened world as though it were alright. Day and night our beings will cry out for the new Day of His appearing to come. We will mourn until that Day.

At His Return, Jesus desires that we would be one with His heart. He is the God-Man who is coming to reign as King on the earth. He is coming to make the wrong things right and to overthrow all enemies of darkness that take their stand against Him. What happens when Love Himself comes to earth? He wants to find many on the earth who are in agreement, full agreement, with His love and all it requires, with His hatred of wickedness and love for righteousness.

He will rule in flaming bright-righteousness and love. And when He comes, He comes as Himself. He must be Himself without reservation. And everything that does not come into perfect agreement with all that He is must be destroyed. This is our urgency—to come into union with that Man's heart and be made holy, without any known opposition within. Out of that union we lift our voice, crying out for what He cries out for, refusing to live as though things were alright *until* He reigns as King on earth. The realities of intimacy and urgency are of one reality. *We cry out in urgent intercession because of a burning intimacy that cannot be denied until fullness is realized.*

The Anointing of Anna: Sustained Urgency

Perhaps the greatest wonder of Anna's life was the culmination of years spent in the place of prayer and fasting, day in and day out, *decade after decade, for sixty years continually.* Undoubtedly Anna faced much ridicule from her friends of her earlier years. As she moved out of her twenties and into her thirties, she probably experienced a painful stigma as her friends and relatives would say, "Anna, you've done this long enough. Why don't you get on with the rest of your life?

You're going to waste away in that temple! Anna, what has happened to you?" Yet year after year, day in and day out, she persisted. What kind of inward fire burned in her, what kind of vision was set before her eyes, what kind of love fueled this urgency that persisted for such a prolonged measure of time?

Sustaining a life of prayer and fasting is a combination of the *grace of the Lord* at work on the heart and the *response of the believer* to remain *fueled* by an inward fire of love for God and *far* from the spirit of slumber and dullness that so readily grows in the human heart.

First, we must stay connected to the heart of Jesus as our Bridegroom whom we love desperately. Only one truly in love with God can sustain the rigors of this lifestyle. If love and desire for God is not our primary motive in fasting and prayer, we will burn out quickly over time and end up as "burned stones," disillusioned and disconnected at the heart level.

Second, we must resist the dullness that subtly settles in over time, the gradual distance and disconnect at the heart level from the groaning that once stirred so deeply. We have been called to live lives of wakefulness, continuously watching with hearts alert, fighting always the spirit of dullness that seeks to settle in. This does not mean that we live frenzied or fearful; it means we live desperately focused.

> *"You are all sons of the light and sons of the day. We are not of the night nor of darkness. Therefore let us not sleep, as others do, but let us watch and be sober." 1 Thess. 5:8*

Third, we must bear a certain stigma in this calling. The enemy will go to great lengths to sideline us in the place of prayer. He will use the stigma voiced by others that says we should quit being "inactive" and give ourselves to *serving* in ministry, helping people rather than just "checking out" from the true difficulties of life. This is a sure stigma that must be understood and born in the calling of being an "Anna" before the Return of Jesus.

Fourth, we must grasp the role of intercession in God's governmental strategy. Critical to sustaining our urgency in the place of prayer and fasting is a deep understanding of the centrality of prayer in God's government and a continual reconnecting to the nobility of this calling.

Intercessors must know that intercession is the primary means that God has chosen to release His government in the earth. *Finally, we must cultivate a true understanding of God's desire to answer our prayers.* He has called us and anointed us to pray because He desires to answer and bring forth the promises given in His Word in correspondence to a praying Church. We must believe that it is in His heart to really answer.

Friends That Mourn For the Bridegroom

AND JESUS SAID TO THEM, "CAN THE FRIENDS OF THE BRIDEGROOM MOURN AS LONG AS THE BRIDEGROOM IS WITH THEM? BUT THE DAYS WILL COME WHEN THE BRIDEGROOM WILL BE TAKEN AWAY FROM THEM, AND THEN THEY WILL FAST. MT 9:15

Mourning for God and Jesus' Return is our great invitation and the heart posture He would desire us to walk in as friends in this hour. We are to be those who live out a persistent cry, a continual voice lifted in intercession, crying out for His Kingdom to come presently and ultimately. To mourn is to live in the lamenting of Jesus' absence. *It is to live in a continual groan because things are not as they should be.* Things are only ever as they should be in Jesus' presence. It is only when He is here, once again, on the earth that the mourning finally comes to an end. Our mourning gives witness that we are not of this world. And we groan within ourselves, eagerly waiting for the King to come once again and make the wrong things right.

> *...we ourselves groan within ourselves, eagerly waiting for the adoption, the redemption of our body...but if we hope for what we do not see, we eagerly wait for it with perseverance. Rom. 8:23 - 25*

We mourn because things are not right and there is only one Man, in all heaven and earth, who can make them right and He is not here in bodily form. Only when His feet walk once more on the earth, when His voice can be heard by every ear, when He rules from His throne in Jerusalem, ordering and bringing all things under His perfect leadership, only then will things be right. Only then will there be peace and safety. Mourning for God is more than longing in lovesickness or sweet yearnings. *To mourn is to tear the heart. It is to groan in an intercessory cry without consolation until His Appearing.*

> *For the grace of God that brings salvation has appeared...teaching us that, denying ungodliness and worldly lusts, we should live soberly, righteously and godly in this present age, looking for the blessed hope and glorious appearing of our great God and Savior Jesus Christ. Titus 2:13*

It is in the context of this mourning laying hold of the Body of Christ, this Cry ascending on the Church worldwide, that the Father will hear from Heaven and respond by splitting the skies with the Return of the Son. God's invitation to us is that we would partner with Him in this governmental role of intercession, becoming *lives consumed by this all-consuming Cry*, responding to God's grace in lifestyles of prayer and fasting, with the great UNTIL always before us...*UNTIL He comes.*

My House shall be Called the House of Prayer

CHAPTER 4

PRAYING CHURCH PRINCIPLE #1 - Prophetic In the House – *Ears to Hear, and Eyes to See*

*Mat 21:10 And when he was come into Jerusalem, all the city was moved, saying, Who is this? 11 And the multitude said, **This is Jesus the prophet** of Nazareth of Galilee.*

Okay, let's get into the nuts and bolts of how we will go from where we are to where God said we would be - *A House of Prayer for all Nations*. Firstly, in this end-time house of prayer that's being raised up in the earth the predominant ministry gift in the Church will not be the "Pastoral" gift. God is restoring the five-fold ministry gifts back to His end-time House of Prayer. (Eph. 4:12). And He's re-establishing the end-time expression of His church upon the foundation of the Apostles and Prophets, that a complete revelation of Jesus may be seen as the cornerstone of the Church (Eph. 2:20). The day of the gift of "Pastor" being the only gift or predominant gift leading churches and communities of faith and prayer will pass away with the old wineskins. God is raising up Watchmen, that pray more than they say. God is raising up Intercessors that will stand between heaven and what God wants to do in the earth, and bring the two together. When Jesus came into the city, they asked, Who is this? And the multitude said this is *"Jesus the Prophet."* Jesus the Apostolic Prophet will be seen in the church, bringing the church to its' destined place as a house of prayer for all nations.

Prophetic or Pathetic

When we talk about the Prophetic we must distinguish between the prophetic of Jesus the Christ and the prophetic that has been pawned off in the church as prophetic, when it's actually been more pathetic than anything else.   When I say that God is restoring the Prophetic in His House of Prayer, we're not talking about the prophetic that we've seen over the last 20 or 30 years in the church. We're not talking about the prophetic that we've known where a man or woman, we call Prophet or Prophetess, comes in as the superstar special speaker and prophesy's temporal, flesh pleasing, ear tickling prophecies that make you shout or makes your flesh feel good. We have looked to this aspect of the Prophetic gift to tell us what God is saying, or what we want to hear, devoid of us having to seek God for ourselves. We have replaced the true New Covenant function of the Prophet with an old covenant mix that has produced a spiritually lazy, bored believer. We should always keep in mind that; *Prophets do not replace my need to hear from God for myself. And my need to hear from God for myself does not replace my need for Prophets."*

The Coming of 21st Century Seers

When I speak of God restoring the Prophetic in His House of Prayer, what I'm speaking about is men and women that can see and hear in the spirit for themselves. I'm speaking about the function of the prophetic in every believer. This end-time prophetic that's going to be seen in the church that prepares the way of the Lord is a prophetic that sees and hears in the Spirit, by the Spirit. It's not going to be an elitist mentality on this prophetic gift whereby we look to one man to know what God is saying. But it's going to be the raising up of servant prophets. Amos 3:7 *Surely the Lord GOD will do nothing, but he reveals his secrets unto his servants the prophets.* In this end-time church God is going to raise up servants that are prophets, not just preachers, or pulpiteers, but housewives, husbands, mothers, fathers, businessmen, actors, producers, politicians, men and women that are able to see God and hear from God for themselves. This prophetic move in the 21st century church will not just be one man prophesying or people going around giving everybody they see personal prophesies, but it's going to produce a culture of each believer seeing and hearing from God for themselves. It's not going to be a church where there is just one man that sees and hears from God, and comes back and tells everyone what God is saying. But he's going to raise up servant prophets in answer to Moses' prayer that all God's people were prophets, with the spirit of Moses, as is recorded in Numbers 11:25-29.

To Seek God for Yourself You Must Learn To Hear From God for Yourself

The prophetic and the house of prayer go hand in hand because prayer and hearing from God are inseparable. When you can't hear from God for yourself, you don't pray when you need God, you go looking for someone to pray for you. You go looking for someone you think can get a prayer through. When you can't hear from God for yourself, you don't pray when you need God, you go looking for someone to preach you a sermon, or someone to give you a word in a church service, not a prayer service. The reason why people in the modern church don't pray any more than they do now is because we don't really believe God is listening to us, because we have not been taught how to hear God speak to us in response to our prayers. We don't really know how to hear from God. We have been told that only the Pastor can hear from God. So we have to wait on the Pastor to tell us what God is saying. We have to wait on the Pastor to tell us what to do, when to do it, and how to do it.

However, the essence of prayer requires that you hear God speak to you in response to your speaking to Him. ***Prayer is you speaking to God and telling Him what He tells you to tell Him. Prayer is God placing on your heart what's on His heart so that His will can be done in earth, as it is in heaven.*** You can't say you pray and you don't hear from God. That's like saying you can talk but you can't hear. Nine times out of ten if you're dumb and can't talk in the natural, it's because you can't hear. Many times dumbness comes from being deaf, or having some sort of hearing problem. Speaking to and hearing from God are inseparable. If you speak to God it's because you've heard him. It takes faith to speak to God, and faith cometh by hearing and hearing comes by the word of God.

> *He that cometh to God must believe that he is and that he is a rewarder of them that diligently seek him. (Hebrews 11:6)*

So the prophetic, speaking to and hearing from God, and the Church being returned to a house of prayer will go hand in hand in the end-time church with this new wineskin. It's one of the main principles that will establish God's house as the house of prayer. It will cause people to want to engage God's heart in prayer consistently day and night. It's because of their ability through the power of the prophetic, to finally hear from God for themselves that will turn them on to prayer. In this coming expression of the House of Prayer for all Nations we will begin to seek and see God for ourselves and our prayer meetings will go from empty bored prayers of drudgery and work, to joyous prayer meetings of worship and fascination with God's beauty. We will speak, sing and worship our interaction and dialogue with God causing us to encounter the glorified Christ in our prayer meetings. Leaders that see the glorified Christ with eyes that have been sanctified to behold the glory and beauty of Christ will lead the body of Christ into the glory, beauty realm of God at the end of the age. This will cause the church to be fascinated and exhilarated with the Glorified Christ, thusly seeking to become a Glorified Church.

The Global Outpouring Of The Spirit Of Prophecy In The End Times – Guidelines For Prophetic Ministry

> [17] *In the last days...I will pour out of my spirit on <u>all flesh</u>; your sons and your <u>daughters</u> shall prophesy, your <u>young</u> men shall see visions, your old men shall dream dreams.* [18] *I will pour out my spirit...* [20] *<u>before</u> the coming of the great and awesome day of the lord. (acts 2:17-20)*

<u>All flesh</u>: All are called to prophesy and function in the gifts of the Spirit. All men (not just prophets), women (not just men), children (not just adults), and all nations (not just Israel).

> [5] *I wish you <u>all</u> spoke with tongues...even more that you <u>prophesied</u>...* [31] *You can <u>all prophesy</u>. (1 Cor. 14:5, 31)*
>
> [7] *The manifestation of the Spirit is given to <u>each one</u> for the profit of all. (1 Cor. 12:7)*

<u>Before</u>: The day of the Lord refers to Jesus' second coming. The day of Pentecost was only a down payment of a far greater fulfillment of this prophecy in the end times before Jesus' return.

What Is Prophecy?

Prophecy is the testimony of Jesus and is the revelation of what is on His heart for His people.

> [10] *For the <u>testimony of Jesus</u> is the spirit of prophecy. (Rev. 19:10)*

Most prophecy is "human words reporting something that God brings to mind" (Wayne Grudem). The Spirit conveys to our mind thoughts we communicate in contemporary language. They are a mixture of God's words and man's words that combine divine inspiration and with the human process. Some prophetic words may be 10% God's words and 90% man's word while others have a greater revelatory content. Most prophecy has a strong mixture of man's ideas

The first rule of prophetic ministry is that it must always <u>honor the written word of God</u>.

The prophetic spirit can be manifested in dramatic ways or in very subtle ways. The dramatic ways include experiencing an open vision, angelic encounter, the audible voice of the Lord or a prophetic dream. Prophecy is released in us most often by faint impressions given by the Spirit.

Three Levels Of Prophetic Ministry

Office of the prophet: They have a track record in regularly prophesying with accuracy about the future. They regularly receive open visions, angelic visitations, God's audible voice, and detailed information such as names, dates, and future events, and are used in the power gifts (healing and miracles). They give correction or direction to the body (by going through the leadership team). All believers are called to prophesy (1 Cor. 14:39), however not all are prophets (1 Cor. 12:29).

Prophetic ministry: They receive helpful prophetic words on a regular basis and occasionally receive higher levels of revelation as a prophet (open visions, angelic visitations, God's audible voice, and detailed information such as names, dates, and future events) with the power gifts.

Simple prophecy: This is for edification, exhortation, and comfort of people by giving them the prophetic impressions that they have received. Usually these words are given in a small group setting or in a ministry line instead of on the microphone in a public meeting.

> [3] *He who prophesies speaks <u>edification</u> and <u>exhortation</u> and <u>comfort</u> to men. (1 Cor. 14:3)*

Edification: Building up people by giving **_confirmation_** that brings them hope or focus. A common way to do this is by giving them a Scripture that has been important to them or by confirming their ministry calling (evangelist, school teacher, marketplace, etc.).

Exhortation: calling people to **_persevere_** in their ministry calling or promises, etc.

Comfort: speaks of giving God's **_perspective_** in a time of difficulty or uncertainty

The Difference Between Old Testament And New Testament Prophecy

Few or many: In the OT there were only a few prophets for Israel and thus, the whole world. With the outpouring of the Spirit, the gift of prophecy was widely dispersed. In the OT there is "prophetic concentration" of a few prophets. In the NT there is "prophetic distribution" of many.

100% accuracy: The OT ground rules for prophets was 100% accuracy and was required upon the penalty of death (Deut. 18:20). The NT requires the prophets to judge each other's words (1 Cor. 14:29, 1 Thes. 5:19-21). With a number of prophets in each geographic location, the same accuracy is not demanded in the NT with the safeguard of prophets judging one another's words.

> ²⁹ *Let two or three prophets speak, and let the others judge. (1 Cor. 14:29)*

Prophesying by faith: Instead of prophesying only by direct revelation, we prophesy according to the measure of our faith. Thus, we might mix up God's ideas with our words and thoughts.

> ⁶ *Let us prophesy in proportion to our faith... (Rom. 12:6)*

National leaders: OT prophets prophesied regularly to kings. Whereas, most NT prophets spoke to believers rather than to the national leaders of their day.

Administrating Prophecy

There are 3 components of administrating prophecy: revelation, interpretation, and application. The Lord often uses a team of prophetic people to administrate prophetic revelation.

Revelation: refers to receiving the prophetic **information** (the impression, dream, vision, etc.)

> ⁹ *For we know in part and we prophesy in part. (1 Cor. 13:9)*

Interpretation: This refers to **understanding** the revelatory information. Even with accurate revelation, it is easy to get a wrong interpretation of it. There are often symbolic elements to visions and dreams, etc. Often we do not understand the revelation until the circumstances unfold that bring its fulfillment. Some give in to the temptation to manufacture the interpretation before it is clear. Ironically, some who are best at receiving a revelation seem worst at interpreting it.

> ⁶ *He (God) said, "Hear My words: If there is a prophet among you, I, the LORD, make Myself known to him in a vision; I speak to him in a dream.*

> [7] *Not so with My servant Moses...8 I speak with him <u>face to face,</u> <u>even plainly,</u> and not in <u>dark sayings</u>..."(Num. 12:6-8)*

<u>Application</u>: This refers to the **<u>wisdom</u>** to rightly apply the information that is interpreted. I recommend asking the following questions: Who is supposed to share the prophetic word? Who is supposed to hear it, the leaders, some individuals, the intercessors or the whole church? How much of it is to be shared, 30% or 100%? When should it be shared? Why? What is the desired impact? The main question is, "What will bring about the maximum amount of edification?"

Functioning In The Spiritual Gifts

<u>Principle</u>: The demonstration of the Spirit's power often follows the **declaration of God's word** from the lips of a believer. The Spirit moves as we **speak words** that agree with God's will.

Prophetic information is given most often in subtle ways in receiving **<u>faint impressions</u>** such as:

1) <u>Mental pictures</u>: reoccurring impressions or pictures in our minds that indicate how the Lord will touch others by imparting His grace or healing to them

2) <u>Emotional stirrings</u>: feeling various emotions like joy, sadness, or a burden for a person or a ministry as an indicator that the Lord will touch others related to that emotion or burden

3) <u>Sympathetic pains</u>: feeling pain in a specific part of our bodies as an indicator that the Lord desires to heal the disease or pain that others are feeling in that particular part of their body

4) *Physical sensations:* experiencing the Spirit's presence (heat, energy, fire, wind, etc.) in a specific area of our bodies or through our five senses (e.g. smell or taste) as an indicator that the Lord desires to touch others in a way related to the physical sensation that we received.

We must be intentional about receiving the Spirit's prophetic leading when we gather in large or small groups or in social gatherings. We do this simply by asking the Spirit, ***"What are You doing or saying?"*** He will often answer by giving us faint prophetic impressions.

> [19] *The Son can do <u>nothing</u> of Himself, but <u>what He sees the Father do</u>... (Jn. 5:19)*

We often do not have prophetic impressions simply because we do not ask for them (Jas. 4:2). Ask the question: "Spirit, what are You saying or doing?" The simple act of asking makes us receptive and attentive to what He is doing and postures us to receive the Spirit's impressions.

> [2] *Yet you do not have <u>because you do not ask</u>. (Jas 4:2)*

I compare functioning in the prophetic to putting up the sail in a boat on a lake on a calm day. When it seems there is no breeze, the sail catches even the most gentle breeze that barely moves the boat. Yet, it moves! A similar dynamic occurs when we ask Jesus what He is doing. Put your sail up by saying, "Holy Spirit, what do You want to do or say through me today?"

The gifts often begin as the <u>still small voice of God</u> or as a subtle impression of the Spirit to our spirit. It can be so subtle that many do not value it. Thus, they ignore it as they wait for an open vision. As they understand and value God's still small voice to them, they will be attentive to it.

> [11] *Behold, the LORD passed by, and a great and strong <u>wind</u> tore into the mountains and broke the rocks in pieces before the LORD, but the LORD was not in the wind; and after the wind an <u>earthquake</u>, but the LORD was not in the earthquake;* [12] *and after the earthquake a <u>fire</u>, but the LORD was not in the fire; and after the fire <u>a still small voice</u>. (1 Kgs. 19:11-12)*

First, we function in the gifts by ***giving expression*** to the impressions that the Spirit gives us. These impressions are like a key that unlocks a door. It requires faith to speak them.

Second, we ***dial down emotionally*** or quiet our soul to "listen" or discern the impressions of the Spirit when we are praying for people. This is opposite to stirring our soul up with fervor when ministering to people. Don't "preach your prayers" over those that you minister to.

Third, we must ***value the power of God*** even when it is released in small measures. We must not despise the smaller measures. It is still God's power that works when even 10% of someone's headache is healed. It is not the work of the devil or human ability. We honor it as such and do not despise it.

We are grateful for every good thing from God's hand. In our pride, we can despise the smallness of God's power in ministry. Some are only interested in God's power when it is manifest in a dramatic measure. They want to walk in the prophetic on their terms. It takes humility to walk with God on His terms of being faithful and grateful in the days of smallness.

Fourth, do not be preoccupied with the ***fear of missing it***. We should be more concerned with never functioning in the gifts! The more important question is not "What if I miss it?" but rather "What if I miss a chance to release God's power to someone in need?"

Fifth, be ***supernaturally natural*** without drawing undue attention to the fact that we are prophesying. We encourage people to prophesy in a way that is dialed down emotionally and without an overemphasis on saying, "thus says the Lord" or the "Lord told me" and to use a humble style that is less melodramatic. It's better to be less dramatic in our prophesying and more helpful to the people. We can say, "I want to pray for you; I believe God wants to touch you." If we are wrong we will not hurt anyone if we use softer language.

Why do believers neglect to prophesy? It takes love and spiritual vigor to prophesy often. Why? It requires ***attentiveness*** to the Spirit to receive small impressions from Him. It also requires ***energy*** and that we take ***risks*** to act on the impressions. It is easier to draw back from all this. There is an intensity involved in being continually available to the Spirit. To be attentive implies refusing the indulgence of anxiety and self-pity that cause so much emotional traffic.

Practical Guidelines For Prophetic Ministry

People must have an attitude of "open expectancy" related to the fulfillment of a prophecy. The exact way that God brings about a word in our lives is often very different than how we envision. We encourage people to put revelations "on the shelf" until you have a clear interpretation.

We ask all to write their prophecies down to give to the leadership team

Have the integrity and humility to clean up any messes that are caused by wrong prophecies.

Create a safe atmosphere so people can grow in their confidence (small group settings). One way is to communicate on paper (so that new comers into your community are informed) the guidelines that your leadership has in giving and receiving prophecy.

Give mercy to those with a teachable spirit. Allow for the risk and accept the inevitability of being humbled as a congregation as you grow in the prophetic. The oxen that bring strength to the farm also bring a mess to the stable. Some prefer to have clean stables even if it means losing the strength that the prophetic ministry brings.

> [4] *Where no oxen are, the trough is clean; but much increase comes by the strength of an ox. (Proverbs 14:4)*

Paul taught that prophets could control their spirit instead of claiming that they "could not help" what they did. One of the fruits of the Spirit is self-control (Gal. 5:22-23).

> [29] *Let two or three prophets speak...*[30] *If anything is revealed to another...let the first keep silent...*[32] *The*

> *spirits of the prophets are subject to the prophets.*
> [33] *God is not the author of confusion but of peace...* [40] *Let all things be done decently and in order. (1 Cor. 14:29-33, 40)*

Prophetic Praying with Music from Intimacy with God

When we talk about the prophetic we are speaking of 3 vital aspects to the prophetic that will release new dimensions of intimacy and connection with God in prayer. These aspects of the prophetic will take our prayer meetings from the boring "rock pile" prayer meetings that are not attended, but by the faithful few, to the joyous vibrant prayers of the multitudes to be refreshed in the presence of God. These 3 aspects of the prophetic are;

- Prophetic hearing – Rev. 2:7 *He who has an hear to hear*
- Prophetic seeing – Hab. 2:2-4 *Write this vision.....*
- Prophetic singing – Eph 5:19 *Speaking in songs, hymns..*

Prayer that is joyous and able to be enduring and refreshing is prayer that is done with music out of love and intimacy with Jesus. Only when we pray from the place of intimacy with Jesus and with music will we be able to pray day and night with perseverance and persistence. (Luke 18:7, 8) This type of praying is referred to as worshipping prayer that releases the Spirit of Prophecy. Praise and Worship is actually the first level of Prayer. Jesus taught His disciples to pray by instructing them to access their time in prayer with God the father by saying, "***Hallowed be thy Name,*** *Thy Kingdom come thy will be done, in earth as it is in Heaven.* (Matt. 6:10) Worship of the name of God in earth gives access for heaven to come to earth, causing us to experience the beauty and magnificence of heaven on earth.

CHAPTER 5

PRAYING CHURCH PRINCIPLE #2 Purity in the House - The 7 steps to cleansing the temple – Revelation 2, 3

> *Mat 21:12 And Jesus went into the temple of God, and **cast out all them that sold and bought in the temple**, and overthrew the tables of the moneychangers, and the seats of them that sold doves, ...he that hath an ear to hear let him hear what the spirit says to the church.*

The prophetic spirit of the Lord in prayer is what will take the church from its religious and ceremonial place in society to **its place of purity** power and praise in the earth. When Jesus came into the religious ceremonial temple of his day he saw a whole lot corruption. He saw a system of corruption, a system of manipulation. And he went into the temple and cast out all that sold and bought in the temple and overthrew the tables of the moneychangers and the seats of them that sold doves and said; *"My house shall be called a House of Prayer but you have made it a den of thieves."*

In order for God's house to become a house of prayer we're going to have to become a place of purity. Jesus, once again, is going to have to cleanse the church from corrupt systems she's relied on and allowed to operate within the 21st century church. Corrupt financial systems, corrupt hierarchal systems of operation between the Clergy and laity, corrupt educational systems, corrupt moral and sexual abuse issues within the 21st century church, are all going to have to be purified. Many churches will be unable to transition into this House of prayer paradigm where prayer is prioritized over board meetings, budget meetings, and planning meetings, because to them the church has become a big business where they have learned how to run the church without God's wisdom. It would be difficult for them not to look at their systems of budgets and systems of cash flow and R.O.I- *rate of return,* credits and debits and not feel like they have to do something to make something happen when it's not adding up. However in the end times it's not going to add up. In the end time house of prayer there will be one source of supply and provision- PRAYER. There will be one main business of the house of God – PRAYER. If God doesn't provide we'll not have it.

It's the prophetic word that's going to cast out man made systems of manipulation and control established by corrupt leaders in a corrupt system. In this end-time prophetic church that returns to its purpose as a house of prayer she will once again live by every word that proceeds out of the mouth of God. Jesus shows us how to live during times of persecution and affliction from the enemy in Matthew 4, and Luke 4. *But he answered and said, It is written, Man shall not live by bread alone, but by every word that proceeds out of the mouth of God.*

He That Hath An Ear To Hear.......*The Purifying Of The 21ˢᵗ Century Church Through The Messages* To The 7 Churches Of Asia

In the last days, Jesus is going to release to his church a hearing ear like no other time in church history, so that he that hath an ear to hear will be able to hear what the Spirit is saying to His church. 8 times in the gospels and 8 times in the book of the revelation Jesus said.......*he that hath an ear to hear let him hear what the spirit says to the church.* Seeing and hearing in the spirit is what's going to purify His church for the unique dynamics of the end-times, and the coming of the Lord.

It's through this hearing ear of the prophetic that the church will be cleansed. The prophetic dimension comes not only to bring direction but it comes to bring correction. Correction must come before direction. When the Lord becomes our Shepherd again in his church, Psalm 23:3 ....*Thy Rod (correction) and thy Staff (direction, and protection) will comfort us* The word comfort in the Hebrew text is the word na^cham, which not only means to pity, console, and ease, but it also means to repent. When the Lord becomes our Shepherd, his rod, his correction and his staff, direction and protection will cause us to repent and be led by the spirit. With the rod of correction those that know the voice of their shepherd will repent of those things that the spirit reveals and receive comfort as a part and parcel of the prophetic anointing that comes to purify, purge and process us through the wilderness to the promised land of green pastures. This is what the process of purifying will produce. This process was seen by Jesus in correcting the churches of Asia in John's Revelation of Jesus to the seven churches.

He Who Has an Ear Let Him Hear: 5 Implications

As I stated above, the exhortation that Jesus repeated the most in His earthly ministry was the call to have ears to hear what the Spirit is saying. This is written 16 times (8x in the Gospels and 8x in Revelation (Mt. 11:15; 13:9, 43; Mk. 4:9, 23; 7:16; Lk. 8:8; 14:35; Rev. 2:7, 11, 17, 29; 3:6, 13, 22; 13:9).

> [7] *He who has an ear, let him hear what the Spirit says to the churches. (Rev. 2:7)*

First, it signaled that the truth being proclaimed was *extremely important to Jesus.*

Second, Jesus is saying that *there is more than* what is obvious. He is calling us to pursue the deeper truth being set before us and not to be content to understand only what is on the surface.

Third, it takes the *supernatural help of the Holy Spirit* to grasp it. The unaided mind of even a devoted believer will not be able to automatically comprehend the truth being set forth. Jesus is making it clear that it is beyond our natural ability. Jesus wants us to ask the Spirit for help.

Fourth, each time Jesus spoke this exhortation in Revelation it was about their *eternal rewards and destiny*. He warned them and us to have ears to hear because it takes supernatural insight to grasp them. When reading each reward, pray; "Lord, show me more".

Fifth, it takes a *focused determination* to lay hold of the truths being referred to. We do not automatically respond to them in a deep and sustained way to them. It will take a tenacious commitment to maintain these truths in our lives long-term because of our propensity to lose touch with them.

Jesus started by speaking to individuals ("he" who has an ear) then changed to addressing a group (the "churches"). There is an individual and a corporate response that the Spirit desires. Jesus was the only one in the NT to give this exhortation. He echoed Moses who called Israel to "hear" meaning to "have ears to hear" (Deut. 6:4-5) and the Father (Ps. 45:10).

> ^{4} *Hear, O Israel: The LORD our God, the LORD is one! 5 You shall love the LORD your God with all your heart, with all your soul, and with all your strength. (Deut. 6:4-5)*

A Revelation of the Glorified Christ to His Church

Revelation is called the "revelation of Jesus" because it reveals His heart, power and leadership.

> ^{1} *The Revelation of Jesus Christ, which God gave Him (Jesus) to show His servants. (Rev. 1:1)*

The theme of Revelation is Jesus returning to take leadership of the earth in partnership with His people to reap a harvest of souls (Rev. 7:9) and replace all governments (Rev. 11:15; 19:15-16).

> *⁷ Behold, <u>He is coming with clouds</u>, and every eye will see Him... (Rev. 1:7)*

Rev. 2-3: Jesus gives us the clearest picture of what He wants in the Church in His seven letters where He exhorts believers to be over comers. Rev. 2-3 is key to forming the end-time prayer and prophetic movement. Jesus will come ONLY in context to a prepared Bride in unity with the Spirit and anointed in prayer to release God's glory on earth and to release the Tribulation to confront darkness.

> *⁷ For the marriage of the Lamb has come, and His wife has <u>made herself ready</u>. (Rev. 19:7)*

> *¹⁷ The Spirit and the Bride say, "Come!" (Rev. 22:17)*

> *⁴ <u>The prayers of the saints</u>, ascended before God...5 Then the angel took the censer, filled it with <u>fire from the altar</u>, and threw it to the earth... (Rev. 8:4-5)*

The Jn. 14:12 prayer anointing of *"greater works than these shall we do,"* involves the miracles of Exodus and Acts being combined and multiplied on a global level to loose revival and the Tribulation and to bind the Antichrist.

> *Most assuredly, I say to you, he who believes in Me, the works that I do he will do also; and greater works than these he will do, because I go to My Father. (Jn. 14:12)*

> *On this rock I will <u>build My church</u>, and the gates of Hades shall not prevail against it. 19 And I will give*

> *you the keys of the kingdom of heaven, and*
> *<u>whatever you bind on earth</u> will be bound in*
> *heaven, and <u>whatever you loose on earth</u> will be*
> *loosed in heaven. (Mt. 16:18-19)*

As Jesus revealed himself in his glorified state to John the Revelator, Jesus is going to reveal himself to his church in the 21st century to purify and prepare His church for the unique dynamics of the end-times and the coming of the Lord. Hearing from and seeing the glorified Christ is the prerequisite for the Church receiving purity and positioning to be prepared as a bride for her husband, not having spot, wrinkle, blemish or any such thing. Her purity is going to come as she is ushered into the presence of the Christ of the lamp stands and are shown things that are, was and are to come. The Church of the 21st century that gets a revelation of Jesus Christ like was given to John will see and hear things from the seven Spirits of God which are before the throne

> *Rev 1:1 The Revelation of Jesus Christ, which God*
> *gave unto him, to show unto his servants things*
> *which must shortly come to pass; and he sent and*
> *signified it by his angel unto his servant John: 2*
> *Who bare record of the word of God, and of the*
> *testimony of Jesus Christ, and of all things that he*
> *saw. 3 Blessed is he that reads, and they that hear*
> *the words of this prophecy, and keep those things*
> *which are written therein: for the time is at hand. 4*
> *John to the seven churches which are in Asia: Grace*
> *be unto you, and peace, from him which is, and*
> *which was, and which is to come; and from the*
> *seven Spirits which are before his throne; 5 And*
> *from Jesus Christ, who is the faithful witness, and*
> *the first begotten of the dead, and the prince of the*
> *kings of the earth. Unto him that loved us, and*
> *washed us from our sins in his own blood, 6 And*

80

> hath made us kings and priests unto God and his
> Father; to him be glory and dominion forever and
> ever. Amen.

A Vision of the Church without Spot or Wrinkle

What John saw of Jesus in chapter 1 of the revelation caused John to get a revelation of the church in chapter 2 the way Jesus created it to be, without spot, or wrinkle or any such thing, holy and without blemish. John received the word that would wash the church from her compromise, sin, doctrinal error, and her weaknesses. The first things John saw after he was translated by the Spirit to the Lord's Day was Jesus revealed in the seven golden candlesticks. The seven golden candlesticks represent the church as the light of the world. The seven candlesticks also represent the outpour of the Holy Spirit in seven dimensions that will cause the church to maneuver through the unique dynamics of the end-times. When the church becomes a house of Prayer and begins to hear and see in the spirit, they will begin to hear the voice as a trumpet that will signal a shift and a pouring out of His spirit to bring light, and illumination to the church.

> *Rev 1:10 I was in the Spirit on the Lord's day, and heard behind me a great voice, as of a trumpet, 11 Saying, I am Alpha and Omega, the first and the last: and, What thou seest, write in a book, and send it unto the seven churches which are in Asia; unto Ephesus, and unto Smyrna, and unto Pergamos, and unto Thyatira, and unto Sardis, and unto Philadelphia, and unto Laodicea.12 And I turned to see the voice that spake with me. And being turned, I saw seven golden candlesticks;*

The Seven Golden Candlesticks – The Seven Spirits of God to lead the church through tribulation

The seven golden candlesticks represents the seven spirits of God which will be poured out on the church (the perfected body of Christ) that will cause the church of the 21st century to be able to operate in and through persecution in the end-times, causing her to thrive not just survive, causing her to be raised up, not brought down, to come out victorious, not be overcome or defeated by the enemy. These seven spirits of God that will be seen by the Church is what will cause the church to transition into her end-time and eternal destiny as a House of Prayer for all nations. These seven spirits seen by John with Jesus standing in the midst of His church are recorded in Isaiah 11: 2

> *Isa 11:2 And the spirit of the LORD shall rest upon him, the spirit of wisdom and understanding, the spirit of counsel and might, the spirit of knowledge and of the fear of the LORD; 3 And shall make him of quick understanding in the fear of the LORD: and he shall not judge after the sight of his eyes, neither reprove after the hearing of his ears: 4 But with righteousness shall he judge the poor, and reprove with equity for the meek of the earth: and he shall smite the earth with the rod of his mouth, and with the breath of his lips shall he slay the wicked. 5 And righteousness shall be the girdle of his loins, and faithfulness the girdle of his reins.*

1. The Spirit of the Lord - Jesus Christ
2. The Spirit of Wisdom
3. The Spirit of Understanding
4. The Spirit of counsel
5. The Spirit of Might

6. The Spirit of Knowledge
7. The Spirit of the fear of the Lord

Each of these seven spirits will be received by the church during the unique dynamics of the end-times. Each of these seven spirits will be received by the Church that reveals herself in seven characteristics shown in the end-times to empower her to endure to the end to her glorified and purified state as a bride adorned for her husband. These seven spirits seen in the seven golden candlesticks of the Revelation of John is what will cause the church to be a light to the Jews and the world to enlighten the way of the Lord and bring the nations to Jesus.

> *Isa 60:1 Arise, shine; for thy light is come, and the glory of the LORD is risen upon thee. 2 For, behold, the darkness shall cover the earth, and gross darkness the people: but the LORD shall arise upon thee, and his glory shall be seen upon thee. 3 And the Gentiles shall come to thy light, and kings to the brightness of thy rising. 4 Lift up thine eyes round about, and see: all they gather themselves together, they come to thee: thy sons shall come from far, and thy daughters shall be nursed at thy side. 5 Then thou shalt see, and flow together, and thine heart shall fear, and be enlarged; because the abundance of the sea shall be converted unto thee, the forces of the Gentiles shall come unto thee.*

The end-time Church will operate in these seven spirits seen as lights in the seven golden candlesticks. Jesus will be in the midst of her, leading her through the valley and the shadow of death as their shepherd, His rod and staff comforting them, preparing a table before her in the presence of her enemies. Again, In order for Him to lead us in direction with His staff through the end times, He's going to have to correct us with His rod, enabling us to follow him through this valley and shadow of death. This correcting of His Church is necessary for the church to be purified and led by him in the end-times. Jesus will cleanse and purify his church through the word of admonition and correction he gave to the 7 churches in the Revelation of Jesus Christ. *He that hath an ear the hear let him hear what the Spirit says to the church.*

The Church's Power to Endure and Overcome at the End of the Age

The Book of Revelation is an "Eschatological Book of Acts" revealing the acts of the Spirit through the end-time apostles and prophets and the praying Church under Jesus' authority. Jesus will have partnership with the end-time apostles and prophets in binding and loosing the events in the Book of Revelation as He did with the apostles in the Book of Acts. He defines the spiritual maturity necessary for the Church to release the Great Tribulation by prophetic prayer under His leadership in the way that Moses released the 10 plagues on Egypt and in the way that the apostles established the Church in Acts.

7 Prayers of Repentance for the Church at the end of the age from the 7 churches of Asia

For the body of Christ to be positioned to partner with Jesus for the release of the events in the Book of Revelation she must walk in purity as a bride without spot or wrinkle. To walk as a pure and holy bride we must understand the messages given by Jesus to John for the 7 churches of Asia. We must allow the Holy Spirit to cleanse us of our compromise, weaknesses, and sin as we apply the admonitions to these churches of Asia to the Universal body of Christ at the end of the age. The Spirit of God gave me 7 prayers to pray of repentance in my heart for my life, and family and for intercessory identification for his church, representing this generation of believers, from the 7 churches of Asia in Revelation

2 and 3. Below are these prayers from the revelation given to John of the Church at the end of the age. To read the entirety of this revelation on these 7 churches, you can order my book on Amazon.com, *"Church Without Spot of Wrinkle - 7 steps to becoming a pure and spotless bride, ready for the day of the Lord."*

The 7 Churches of Asia - Revelation 2 & 3

Write the things which thou hast seen, and the things which are, and the things which shall be hereafter; Rev 1:19

1. The Church Of Ephesus. *Rev. 2:4 Nevertheless I have somewhat against thee, because thou hast left thy first love.* **Prayer of Repentance: Jesus I repent for leaving my first love** (*An intimate relationship with Jesus Christ*). I will return to intimacy with you, loving you with all my heart, mind, soul and strength, spending time with you as my first defense against the temptation to work or serve for your acceptance, and against the temptation of the lust of the flesh, the lust of the eyes, and the pride of life. <u>Lord, I turn back to seeking your face. I turn to studying the bridal paradigm of your heart and emotions of love for us as your bride found in the Song of Solomon. I covenant to keep a sacred charge for personal and corporate prayer times in prayer room gatherings in your body, to intercede for your church to return the first commandment to Love you with all our heart, mind, soul and strength, to first place in our midst.</u>

2. The Church Of Smyrna - *Rev 2:10 Fear none of those things which thou shall suffer: behold, the devil shall cast some of you into prison, that ye may be tried; and ye shall have tribulation ten days: be thou faithful unto death, and I will give thee a crown of life.* **Prayer of Repentance: Jesus I repent for the fear of suffering tribulation** and turn to the faithfulness of Christ unto death. (Matt 16:20). <u>Lord, I turn to living and studying to have a mind that is girt with the sufferings of Christ, desiring the fellowship of Christ's sufferings, over the 21st century gospel of comfort and convenience.</u> (1 Peter 4:1-12)

3. The Church Of Pergamos – *Rev 2:14 But I have a few things against thee, because thou hast there them that hold the doctrine of Balaam, who taught Balac to cast a stumblingblock before the children of Israel, to eat things sacrificed unto idols, and to commit fornication.* **Prayer of Repentance: Jesus I repent for allowing the false doctrine of Balaam - (fornication in the church) to operate in my life**. This is the toleration of fornication through the teaching of the Nicoliatans which taught a perversion of the doctrine of liberty, along with Antinomianism, which is the belief that the gospel frees us from obedience to specific moral standards, since we believe that salvation is a gift by faith through grace. Therefore we don't need to repent. <u>Lord, I turn from the spirit of Balaam, eyes of Adultery, and fornication in the church, to spirit of Holiness and sanctification.</u>

4. The Church Of Thyatira – *Rev 2:20 Notwithstanding I have a few things against thee, because thou suffers that woman Jezebel, which calls herself a prophetess, to teach and to seduce my servants to commit fornication, and to eat things sacrificed unto idols.* **Prayer of Repentance: Jesus I repent for allowing the spirit of Jezebel to operate in my life.** (Worshipping false gods of immorality and sorcery) This happens as we look to satisfy the desire for sexual intimacy and spiritual power unlawfully, through sexual immorality and the worship of demon spirits, through the worship of position and authority in his body, the church. These spirits are manifested in the world through drugs, illicit sex and all types of counterfeit power surges, and in the Church it can come on us as a result of preaching, and teaching as a Pastor or leader in Christ's body with the wrong motives, and heart. This is produced many times through a spirit of performance in the church, as well as assuming counterfeit authority. This spirit is also produced through lusting after position in society (political office, etc), and doing whatever is necessary to obtain those offices and positions. Lord I turn from looking to vain and worthless things to satisfy a desire for illegitimate intimacy. I turn from looking to position and authority in ministry, looking for success and fulfillment through leading and building your Church with the wrong motives. I turn to seeking purity of motives and morality, taking a purity covenant with you, and with my wife and children as my accountability partners.

5. The Church Of Sardis – *Rev 3:2 Be watchful, and strengthen the things which remain, that are ready to die: for I have not found thy works perfect before God. 3 Remember therefore how thou hast received and heard, and hold fast, and repent. If therefore thou shalt not watch, I will come on thee as a thief, and thou shalt not know what hour I will come upon thee.* **Prayer of Repentance: Jesus I repent for not watching in prayer** to strengthen the things that remain, allowing the thief to steal our doctrines and faith with the various teachings that seek to avoid persecution. Lord, I turn to the study of these doctrines and teachings of the end-times that I have let slip, and commit my life to teach and preach what the bible teaches about the coming of the Lord as Bridegroom, King and Judge.

6. The Church Of Philadelphia – *Rev 3:7 And to the angel of the church in Philadelphia write; These things says, he that is holy, he that is true, he that hath the key of David, he that opens, and no man shuts; and shuts, and no man opens; 8 I know thy works: behold, I have set before thee an open door, and no man can shut it: for thou hast a little strength, and hast kept my word, and hast not denied my name.* **Prayer of Repentance: Jesus I repent for not pursuing a heart after God and prayer as David** for the keys for opening of doors and windows in heaven. I commit to this 24/7 paradigm of the key of David as revealed to the church of

Philadelphia. This church was given the keys of David to open a door that is shut, and shut doors that should not be opened. Lord, I commit to rebuilding the House of Prayer in the spirit of the Tabernacle of David as your end-time expression of your church as The House of Prayer for all Nations. I commit to establish 24/7 places of worship & prayer in the cities of the earth, culminating in Jerusalem. This is what will enable the church to resist the compromises and the sins represented in the churches of Asia, and be able to stand before the Lord to receive the seven spirits of God and strength to endure the things that will come in the days ahead right before and during the Day of the Lord.

7. The Church of Laodicea – *Rev 3:15 I know thy works, that thou art neither cold nor hot: I would thou wert cold or hot. 16 So then because thou art lukewarm, and neither cold nor hot, I will spue thee out of my mouth. 17 Because thou sayest, I am rich, and increased with goods, and have need of nothing; and knowest not that thou art wretched, and miserable, and poor, and blind, and naked:* **Prayer of Repentance: Jesus I repent for being made lukewarm** (through false and perverted doctrines of prosperity.) Lord, I turn from prosperity for our own benefit, or to make ourselves look appealing and desirable to the world, and I commit to give my heart to you as a living sacrifice, and make a vow to you to offer my money to you for the building of your house of prayer, and cities of refuge throughout this nation and world .

Studying the 7 Letters: The Common Elements in the Letters

__Historical context:__ It is important to gain information about the situation that each church was challenged with politically, economically and spiritually.

Jesus strategically selected these 7 churches knowing they would give prophetic insight into preparing the end-time Church.

Affirmation for faithfulness: What they were doing that Jesus valued. Two churches received no affirmation (Sardis and Laodicea).

Rebuke for compromise: What they must not do. Jesus' correction is not rejection. He had things against 3 churches: Ephesus (2:4), Pergamos (2:14) and Thyatira (2:20). Two churches did not receive a correction (Smyrna and Philadelphia). Jesus gave the sternest rebukes for the following compromises; passivity, immorality and idolatry (covetousness and/or sorcery; Col 3:5; Eph 5:5; 1 Cor. 10:20-22). These were enabled by false teachings on grace that did not require repentance.

Exhortation to respond: What they must do. Jesus gave examples of actions that He required. Sometimes the exhortation had an element of warning. The warnings that Jesus gave most were against ***passivity*** (distraction from the First Commandment because of increased blessing that led to busyness) and ***fear*** (persecution/rejection).

Promise for overcomers: As incentive for diligent faithfulness to Jesus. He promised 22 specific eternal rewards (Rev. 2:7, 10, 17, 26; 3:5, 12, 21). Most have a partial fulfillment now with the fullness in the Millennium. Insight into rewards is essential to equip us to stand in pressure.

Revelation of Jesus: In each message, Jesus called attention to specific aspects of His majesty as seen in Rev. 1 that were most needed in the specific situation of each Church. Sixteen different aspects of Jesus' majesty are highlighted in Rev. 2-3. In the next section we will look at each of the aspects of Jesus' majesty, as well as the weaknesses and strengths of each church to be positioned in the Universal Church at the end of the age to become a pure and spotless bride, to be able stand and partner with Christ as a praying church in His plan to transition the earth to the new age.

CHAPTER 6

PRAYING CHURCH PRINCIPLE #3 - Publish in the House – *Developing your Prophetic History*

> Jesus said, *It is written, My House shall be called a house of prayer (Matt 21:12)*

> *Luk 4:4 And Jesus answered him, saying, It is written, That man shall not live by bread alone, but by every word of God.*

After the praying Church principle of purity in the House we must begin to **Publish in the House.** In Matthew 21:12, when Jesus came into Jerusalem to His house of prayer, He not only begins to prophetically cleanse the temple, but Jesus said, **"It is written,"** *My House shall be called a house of prayer.* The end-time prayer movement and the word of God that will establish God's house as a house of prayer go hand in hand in the house of God returning to its prayer purpose. It's not enough to be a watchman, standing our watch in the house of God; we must not only pray for God's house to become a house of prayer we must speak the word of God for this to take place. A watchman is a prophetic intercessor that not only sees what's coming, but speaks and records what he sees coming. The speaking of the word and recording of what's coming is what releases the vision to all those in the present time of the seeing of the vision and to succeeding generations that have not seen what the watchman has seen. Just as much as a person becomes what he's called to be by seeing, he empowers all to become what they're called to become by speaking, and writing what's been seen so that he that reads it may also run with it. When Jesus was in the wilderness he declared to Satan when he tried to tempt him with an imitation or premature fulfillment of the promise of Son-ship, *"IT IS WRITTEN!"* Jesus used what was written in the word to ward off false presentations of God's will and purpose for him as the Son of God. The church that will become a House of Prayer is going to have to use what is written to also ward off the false presentations of the Church of Jesus Christ and get back to our true Identity as a House of Prayer for all Nations. Speaking, writing and reading what's been seen empowers a group of people to run with what's been seen. In Revelation 1:1 Jesus told John;

> *The Revelation of Jesus Christ, which God gave unto him, to shew unto his servants things which must shortly come to pass; and he sent and signified it by his angel unto his servant John: 2 Who bare record of the word of God, and of the testimony of Jesus Christ, and of all things that he saw. 3 Blessed is he that readeth, and they that hear the words of this prophecy, and keep those things which are written therein: for the time is at hand.*

> *Rev 1:9 I John, who also am your brother, and companion in tribulation, and in the kingdom and patience of Jesus Christ, was in the isle that is called Patmos, for the word of God, and for the testimony of Jesus Christ. 10 I was in the Spirit on the Lord's day, and heard behind me a great voice, as of a trumpet, 11 Saying, I am Alpha and Omega, the first and the last: and, What thou seest, write in a book, and send it unto the seven churches which are in Asia; unto Ephesus, and unto Smyrna, and unto Pergamos, and unto Thyatira, and unto Sardis, and unto Philadelphia, and unto Laodicea.*

Watching (praying), speaking, writing and running with the word of God in the vision of prayer is what's going to turn God's house back to her original purpose as a house of prayer.

Having a Written Vision Produces Faith for a Prayer-Filled Life - Habakkuk 2:2-4

> *I will stand upon my watch, and set me upon the tower, and will watch to see what he will say unto me, and what I shall answer when I am reproved.* ***2*** *And the LORD answered me, and said, Write the vision, and make it plain upon tables, that he may run that readeth it.* *3 For the vision is yet for an appointed time, but at the end it shall speak, and not lie: though it tarry, wait for it; because it will surely come, it will not tarry. Hab 2:1*

There's a difference between a vision that has been written and a vision only seen. A vision written produces faith. A Written vision is a faith-filled vision, and it will come to pass. A vision is written because it is too much to contain in the mind, too much to be believed or received and accomplished by one man or even one generation. It is a vision that is so big only God could bring it to pass. My former Pastor often tells the story of a prayer he wrote down in the front of his Bible 30 or so years ago. It went something like this, "Lord in the church that I Pastor, do things so big that everyone will have to look at it and give glory to God, saying, No man could have done this, it had to be God." That Church grew to over 12,000 members, with a television broadcast that became one of the nations' most recognized Christian television programs in the world, seen throughout the nations of the world.

In order for the church to become what God has called her to be in the nations of the world we're going to have to think out of the box, think big, dream big, pray for things so big that it requires faith in God to see it come to pass. A God given vision that comes from God is not just for you but for preceding generations and requires you to write it down and have faith to see it come to pass. This faith is what attracts Gods word and will to come forth concerning his body

Developing your Prophetic History

When I speak of the vision being written I'm speaking of developing your prophetic history. A prophetic history deals with what God has said, or done in your life in the past, that is leading you to what God has purposed and desires to accomplish in your life in the future. The key ingredient in faith to bring to pass God's will is to have, record and understand your prophetic history.

Why Share Prophetic Histories

Scripture exhorts us to remember what God said and did in the past and to teach it to our children. Remembering what God did in our midst helps us to obey and set our hope in Him.

> *2 I will open my mouth in a <u>parable</u>; I will utter <u>dark sayings</u> of old, 3 which...our fathers told us...4 telling to the generation to come...His wonderful works. 5 He <u>established a testimony</u> in Jacob...He commanded our fathers, that they should make <u>them known</u> to their children; 6 that the generation to come...may declare them to their children, 7 that they may <u>set their hope in God</u>, and not forget the works of God, but keep His commandments. (Ps. 78:2-7)*

Some of God's ways are given to us as parables that unfold in a way that enables us, as the years go by, to see more and more significance in what He did in the past. Jesus spoke many things in parables to make *truth more clear* to those who were humble and hungry for more and to make *truth more obscure* for those who were proud and spiritually self-satisfied (Mt. 13:3, 13-17).

> [3] *He spoke many things to them in parables...13 I speak to them in parables, because seeing they do not see, and hearing they do not hear, nor do they understand. (Mt. 13:3, 13)*

Personal prophecy is given to strengthen our resolve to obey God, to be faithful in prayer and to help us keep focused on the specific ministry assignment that God gives us. Prophecy is not a guarantee, but an invitation from God to participate with Him in prayer, faith, and obedience.

> [18] *THIS CHARGE I COMMIT TO YOU, SON TIMOTHY, ACCORDING TO THE PROPHECIES PREVIOUSLY MADE CONCERNING YOU, THAT BY THEM YOU MAY WAGE THE GOOD WARFARE... (1 TIM. 1:18)*

The Father has a vast and glorious storyline for the whole Body of Christ in this generation. He has a specific assignment for each ministry. We all have a small yet significant part to play in His plans. God wants His people to honor and love the whole Church. There is a part of my inheritance in God that I can only receive as I receive from others in the larger Body of Christ. I have been deeply helped through the years by what God has done through other ministries. One such ministry has been IHOP-Kansas City founded by Mike Bickle, where I had the privilege of serving on staff from 2009 to 2012 as an Intercessory Missionary.

IHOP-KC's Prophetic History

IHOP-KC keeps a 24/7 worship sanctuary in obedience to a specific assignment from the Lord. In Cairo, Egypt, September 1982 God spoke these words to Mike Bickle: *I will change the understanding and expression of Christianity in the earth in one generation.*

> *Changing the understanding*: This statement speaks of the way unbelievers will perceive the Church. Today, many see the Church as boring, irrelevant, and non-threatening (Acts 5:11-13).

> *Changing the expression*: This statement speaks of the way the church expresses its life together as a prophetic people of prayer who walk out Sermon on the Mount lifestyles with a forerunner spirit.

God spoke to Mike about *four heart standards* necessary for his future life and ministry. They are not the only values necessary in a New Testament church, but are the *most neglected* ones. In 1996, God corrected his local church, calling them back to these by using the acronym "IHOP."

> 1. <u>Intercession</u>: night and day prayer and worship affects our *time*
> 2. <u>Holiness</u>: the Sermon on the Mount lifestyle affects our *thoughts and attitudes*
> 3. <u>Offerings</u>: extravagant giving by living simply to give more to the harvest affects our *money*
> 4. <u>Prophetic</u>: confidence in God's intervention (provision, protection, direction) and standing boldly in faith for what the Spirit is saying affects our *security and identity* (most difficult)

My House shall be Called the House of Prayer

The Lord said to Mike, "I am inviting you to be a part of a work that will touch the ends of the earth. You have only said yes, but have not yet done it. Many have said yes, but did not do it (persevere for decades)." The Lord said, "Beware lest your brethren steal these from your heart.

In May 1983, the Lord spoke audibly to Mike, *"I will establish 24-hour prayer in the spirit of the tabernacle of David."* One privilege of keeping a 24/7 worship sanctuary is found in drawing near to God. In engaging in this assignment, we minister to God, release His power, and encounter His heart. In worship and prayer, we contend for a breakthrough of His power on our heart, ministry, and in revelation.

> *[15]But the priests…the sons of Zadok, who <u>kept charge of My sanctuary</u> when the children of Israel went astray from Me, they shall come <u>near</u> Me to minister to Me… (Ezek. 44:15)*

On May 7, 1999, the International House of Prayer of Kansas City (IHOP–KC) began with Mike Bickle and twenty full-time "intercessory missionaries," who cried out to God in prayer with worship for thirteen hours each day. Four months later, on September 19, 1999, prayer and worship extended to the full 24/7 schedule.

IHOP–KC is an evangelical missions organization that is committed to praying for the release of the fullness of God's power and purpose, while actively winning the lost, healing the sick, feeding the poor, making disciples, and impacting every sphere of society—family, education, government, economy, arts, media, religion, etc. The vision of IHOP-KC is to work in relationship with the Body of Christ to serve the Great Commission, while seeking to walk out the two great commandments to love God and people. The Lord has called IHOP-KC to be a community of believers committed to God, each other, and to establishing a

24/7 house of prayer in Kansas City—a perpetual solemn assembly gathering corporately to fast and pray, in the spirit of the tabernacle of David.

The Holy Spirit is orchestrating *one great move of God* in this generation. It is comprised of *many smaller ministry movements* that each has a specific ministry assignment. In other words, the end-time prayer movement is made up of many smaller prayer movements. IHOP–KC is one small movement in the midst of the global end-time move of God.

IHOP–KC's "prophetic history" represents a very small part of God's story in this generation. In telling the prophetic history of IHOP-KC, my prayer is that part of IHOP-KC's story will encourage others to believe God for His fullness in their ministry assignment. As each ministry does their small part, others see the big picture of God's puzzle a little more clearly.

My Prophetic History in the Prayer Movement

In 1999 as I was praying about the direction of the body of Christ going into a new decade, century and millennium, God spoke to my heart and began to relate to me His heart and vision for the 21st century church. He began to tell me about a church that I had no grid or paradigm for. I heard something that caused me to check whether I was hearing from the right spirit. I heard, "*In the 21st century church is going to be opened like Wal-Mart, 24hrs a day.*" I felt like I had heard the spirit saying, the church won't be known by its buildings or it's separate, distinct congregations, but that it would be known by the body of believers in whole cities. At the time I was a new Pastor, leading a traditional apostolic storefront Church of 150 people that my Father had started in 1986 in the inner-city of downtown Columbus Ohio. My father led that church for 11years, when in 1997 he installed me as the Pastor and he became the overseer. From 1997 to 1998 we grew

98

from about 35 people to about 150 people, which was a miracle for a traditional storefront Apostolic Oneness Church. However, in 1999 God spoke a verse of Scripture into my heart from Isaiah 43:18, 19 that says;

> *Remember not the former things, neither consider the things of old, Behold I do a New Thing, Now it shall spring forth.* Then he said these words to me. *Brondon, I'm doing a New Thing, but my Church keeps doing the same ole things.*

You must let go of the Old to see the New

I said, "God, tell me how to do this new thing and I'll do it." He said "You won't do it even if I told you!" You were a traditional church goer who grew up from a traditional church boy, and you're now a traditional church preacher. What the church of this generation has shown you is what you're going to do, even if I tell you to do something different. In order for you to do something new you've got to SEE something new. In order to see something new you've got to LET GO OF THE OLD...*Remember not the former things....BEHOLD, I do a New Thing...(Isa. 43:18,19)*

As I stated earlier, I had no grid or paradigm for this type of a church. All I could see was that if I was going to get this new paradigm I was definitely going to have to let go of the former thing. He instructed me to shut down the ministry I was heading up in 1999, but I relented. The whole year of 1999 it was a struggle that almost destroyed my marriage and family. Anytime you keep doing something that God tells you not to do, you will continue on to your own demise. Finally at the end of 1999 I resigned as Pastor of Apostolic Deliverance Church and begin to attend another ministry in my city until further notice, waiting for God to reveal to me the Wal-Mart structure for this New Thing.

Further notice didn't come until the end of 2007 going into 2008, eight years later. By this time I had accepted a position as a staff Pastor at a Large Multi-ethnic Mega Church in my city, and had been on staff there since 2001. While serving at this Mega-church I had gone from taking a position as the janitor at the church, to take care of my family, after resigning from Apostolic Deliverance Church, to being a staff Pastor overseeing their whole Outreach department of over 300 volunteers, as well as preaching about once a month to the congregation that numbered about five thousand. Things were exploding in my life and ministry. We went on to establish 4 inner-city satellite churches from that ministry, where we saw over 10,000 people saved from all walks of life. We were hosting daily early Morning Prayer meetings at 5am with hundreds of people, and weekly all night prayer meetings every Friday night that was changing the very fabric of our inner city. I was invited several times to the Mayor's office in our city of 1.6 million people to help with our city-wide initiative to curtail crime and lawlessness in the inner-city. Because I had been hosting inner-city tent crusades where whole gangs were being saved and whole projects were being transformed the Police chief had my number and would call me to help them anytime there was a disturbance in these communities. The Mayor offered to give me access to all of the city's recreation centers to turn them into Hope Centers. I was traveling all over the world preaching and telling of what God was doing in bringing revival to our city through our inner-city Outreach ministry.

A Dream of a 21st Century Church of Worship, Entertainment & the Arts

In the middle of all that was happening in my city God spoke to my heart and said this is nothing compared to what I'm about to do in the days to come. Don't get satisfied or comfortable with this. This is still not it. I'm going to do a new thing in the structure of the church to enable her to be able to carry my glory in the earth as it is in heaven. He said, the church of the 21st century is going to see my glory like she has never seen recorded in all of church History. He once again showed me Wal-Mart being opened 24hrs a day 7 days a week and said when my glory comes you won't be able to shut the doors of the church, day or night. He then backed it up with a scripture from Isaiah 60:1-11, *Arise, shine; for thy light is come, and the glory of the LORD is risen upon thee. 11 Therefore thy gates shall be open continually; they shall not be shut day nor night.*

After that encounter, I was visited with a dream at the end of 2007. In the dream I saw *a hybrid Worship, Arts and Entertainment, 24hr prayer ministry* taking place in the building of my father's old store front church in downtown Columbus in the center of the city. It had people coming at all times of the day and night to worship and offer their gifts back to God. There were so many people coming to that little place in the inner-city that we had to move all the chairs out to contain the people, and they were still lined up miles down the street waiting to get into the building. Young people were coming from all over the city signing up to be worship leaders, hip hop rappers, dancers, painters, actors, and musicians, all to offer their good and perfect gifts that come from the Lord back to him for worship, prayer and godly entertainment. That building had so many people coming that we had to keep the doors open day and night 24 hours a day, 7 days a week.

When I woke up I heard God speak the same scripture from 1999, Isaiah 43:19; *Behold I do a new thing, Now it shall spring forth.* Only this time the emphasis wasn't on God doing a New Thing, but on the phrase, *"**NOW**!!! IT SHALL SPRING FORTH."* He spoke in my spirit, this is the NOW SEASON for NEW THINGS. I felt as if he was challenging me and giving me a window of opportunity to break from the Old and into the New all at the same time. As I lamented that I didn't know where to start or how to do what he was challenging me to do, saying, "I haven't seen anything like this before," He said these words: *"Before you can see what I want to do in this new expression of the church in the earth, you must seek the pattern from me, not man. You must build upon my pattern, out of a revelation of who I AM!* I said, how do I know when I've received that revelation? He then said, *"If your revelation or pattern of me in the church does not give my people a desire for intimacy with me through prayer and fasting – A Praying Church model, - this revelation or pattern was not given from my Father which is in heaven, but flesh and blood has revealed it unto you.* He went on to say, *"If the foundation you've built upon does not produce a church of corporate and personal prayer meetings that produce an encounter with the Glorified Christ, it's been built upon another foundation."*

THE CALL into the World Wide Prayer Movement

At the same time in 2008 as I had this dream, and while I was still struggling with resigning, a national speaker and intercessor from Kansas City Missouri came to our church to preach and talk about an upcoming Solemn Assembly prayer gathering in Cincinnati Ohio entitled "The Call." It was due to take place later that week. The founder Lou Engle was preaching at our church. While preaching he looked down to me sitting on the front row to his right and began speaking to me from the platform, saying, ***"Sir I don't know you but I feel I'm here just to preach to you."*** As he was preaching about the pro-life movement being the next movement from the civil rights movement, he begin to talk about God raising up African American prophets to trumpet this message like Dr. Martin Luther King Jr. in the 1960's.

That got my attention, because Dr. Martin Luther King Jr. had been a lifelong mentor of mine, who I had studied extensively for 15 years. Every tape, book, CD, Video, DVD that was out there, I had seen it, read it, and studied it. Dr. Martin Luther King had been the only person I had seen in modern, African-American Christendom that had really lived out the Sermon on the Mount lifestyle in the social order, and had given His life in the process for the cause of ending an unjust system in the earth. He was a preacher that I had seen boldly proclaim a message that he knew would eventually get himself or His family killed, yet he continued to speak and work towards the cause he believed God had given him. All the preachers that I knew were preaching a message that focused on escaping persecution and tribulation. I was raised in the theological foundation of bypassing hard times and persecution, and preached this message, even though I had inclinations and dreams against this thought pattern. I saw no one that exemplified an example of speaking out and taking a stand against an ungodly system regardless of what it cost them. Dr. King had served his generation with the message and life of Agape Love, the Love of God in the heart of men, and was slain for his life's work.

Once this national speaker mentioned this great man of God and said "at the end of the age, many would go forth with the same spirit of boldness and fearlessness in the final generation, confronting false and counterfeit religious and political systems of the Harlot Babylon, I was all ears. Later that week I attended "this mass prayer gathering in a stadium in Cincinnati Ohio with my ministry team, at which time this man of God spotted me in the audience and called me up on the stage to help him pray for the coming together of African Americans and Caucasian ministers. After that event I sought to find out where the man of God was headquartered. Each time we talked we were unable to exchange correspondence. However, I was told that he was headquartered in Kansas City at a place called the International House of Prayer. This was a place I had been recently told by a visitor to our ministry that I should visit. They said because I emphasized prayer as the foundation of the things we did in the inner-city they thought I would really like this prayer ministry in Kansas City.

Well, this speaker being from this ministry was a confirmation that I needed to visit this place called "The International House of Prayer."

In April 2008 I visited I.H.O.P for the first time. When I got there, unbeknownst to me they were in the middle of the Israel Mandate conference. This was another confirmation, because of the calling I've felt to be a missionary to Israel since the early 1990's when I had the privilege to visit Israel. Immediately that got my attention. However, more than anything, what got my attention was the 24hr format of prayer and worship that I witnessed, lining up with the Wal-Mart analogy of the 21st century church. What I saw at IHOP lined up perfectly with the dream I had of worshippers and those gifted and talented in the arts coming into my father's little store front church lined up miles down the road to worship day and night. I was stunned with further confirmation when I found out that IHOP began in 1999 when God first had me close down my father's church for what was coming in the 21st century. WOW! To say I was flabbergasted was a major understatement. I was totally captivated that weekend by everything.

In the midst of the Israel Mandate conference that weekend at IHOP God spoke to me through a speaker from Israel. He said I was going to be coming to Kansas City before I stepped out again to re-open my earthly Father's ministry, and that it would be a 24/7 house of prayer. But he said, *"Go home and wait upon God for the timing."* That was April 2008! It was over a year later, after a year of God walking me step by step off of a worldly system of provision and back to dependency on him, that I resigned in June of 2009. I resigned to begin preparation for this New Thing coming that God had shown me 9 years earlier, the pattern of the 21st century church being established in the earth upon the revelation of Jesus Christ, and as a House of Prayer for all nations.

To prepare for this mandate we moved to Kansas City Missouri on Nov. 20th 2009 to receive a time of training and preparation in establishing the 21st century prototype of the Tabernacle of David, a 24hr House of Prayer for all Nations. We submitted to this call to move to be a part of a unique prayer meeting, a modern day miracle, a ministry that has been in a prayer meeting for over 12 continuous years 24hrs a day, 7 days a week.

The International House of Prayer is truly a sign and wonder in the earth. The Holy Spirit is orchestrating *one great move of God* in this generation. It is comprised of *many smaller ministry movements* that each has a specific ministry assignment. A prophetic history deals with what God has said, or done in your life in the past, that is leading you to what God has purposed and desires to accomplish in your life in the future.

My House shall be Called the House of Prayer

CHAPTER 7

PRAYING CHURCH PRINCIPLE # 4 - Prayer in the House - *Establishing Day & Night Prayers for Justice*

> *and He overthrew the tables of the moneychangers, and the seats of them that sold doves, 13. And said unto them,* **My house shall be called <u>the house of prayer</u>***; but ye have made it a den of thieves*

The Fourth Principle of the Church being restored to the House of Prayer is "*Prayer*" in the House. Prayer in the House of God is the means by which all nations will be reconciled to God, and how justice will be released back to the earth. It's no wonder, when Jesus visited the temple he became so upset with the state of the House of Prayer. It had gotten so far away from what David had established in the tabernacle of David, of 24/7 worship and prayer during His reign. There was little prayer going on, while there was a whole lot of merchandising going on.

Jesus taught that justice would be established through a night and day prayer watch for vengeance against our adversary (speaking God's Word). Justice is God making wrong things right. Jesus is the ultimate social reformer. He was the first to connect justice (social reform and making wrong things right) to night and day prayer.

> *7 Shall God not avenge (bring about justice for, NAS) His elect who cry out day and night to Him? 8 I tell you that He will avenge (bring about justice to, NAS) them speedily. (Lk. 18:7-8)*

The Two sides of God's justice:

1. *Judgment* (punishment, vengeance) to the rebellious who resist God's justice
2. *Salvation* (deliverance, vindication) to the redeemed as He makes wrong things right for them.

Examples of God's justice (judgment/salvation) making wrong things right

1. *Healing:* God's judgment on sickness is seen in the manifestation of healing power

2. *Revival:* God's judgment on compromise is seen in reviving the Church by the Spirit

3. *Soul winning:* God's judgment on the kingdom of darkness is seen when people get saved

4. *End-Time judgments:* God's judgments against the evil governments and their actions

5. *Righteous legislation:* God's judgment on unrighteous legislation (abortion laws, etc.)

6. *Unity (reconciliation):* God's judgment on division in the family, society and the Church

7. *Holiness:* God's judgment on sin, anger, pornography, drugs and rebellion, etc.

Jesus requires night and day prayer as the condition to release justice. Prayer is a very practical expression of the commandment to love one another in that it releases deliverance for the needy.

The House of Prayer: Our Eternal Identity (Isa. 56:7)

Identity of the redeemed: to be God's house that operates by prayer. *7 For My House shall be called a House of Prayer for all nations. (Isa. 56:7)* In Scripture, a person's "house" spoke of their family, resources and future inheritance. The highest identity of the redeemed throughout eternity is to be **"God's House"** or His Family that releases His resources into the natural realm by functioning as a **"House of Prayer"**. We were created to interact deeply with God's heart. God speaks and moves our heart. Then we speak and move His heart. The result is that God's resources are released into the earthly realm.

His resources include wisdom (creative ideas), unity, money, impact, zeal for righteousness, etc. Our identity as sons of God and the Bride of Christ come together in being His Family or House. The Father has ordained that His family rule with Jesus through "intimacy based intercession". God opens doors of blessing and closes doors of oppression in response to our prayers. There are blessings that God has chosen to give, but only as His people rise up in the partnership of prayer.

> *18 The Lord will wait, that He may be gracious to you...19 He will be very gracious to you at the sound of your cry; when He hears it, He will answer you. (Isa. 30:18-19)*

God jealously protects His relationship with us by NOT releasing His resources until we speak to Him in prayer. We must offer specific prayers, not just think about our need with fear, frustration and desperation. He requires that we ask because it causes us to interact with His heart.

> *2 You do not have because you do not ask. (Jas 4:2)*

The Father's resources are strategically withheld to "starve us out of prayerlessness". When the pain of lacking His resources is greater than our busyness then we pray. God knows that our greatness, satisfaction and security are only found in our interaction with His heart in prayer. God requires us to cooperate with Him in the grace of God.

This is an expression of His desire for intimate partnership with us. **God will not do our part** and **we cannot do His part**. If we do not do our part then God withholds some of the help and blessing He would have given us. God has given us a dynamic role in determining some of the measure of the "quality of life".

Prayer tells God what He tells us to tell Him. Many consider this to be too simple and weak to do since everyone can do it. God releases His power in a way that we cannot boast (1 Cor. 1:31). Intercession causes us to internalize God's Word by saying it back to Him many times. Each time we say what God says, it marks our spirit and changes us. Like a computer program may be changed by rewriting each line of code, our inner man is renewed by multitudes of prayers. Intercession draws us in intimacy with His heart while it unifies and transforms us.

Jesus Governs the Universe through His House of Prayer

The governmental center of the universe is the "Prayer Room" which includes all the prayers in heaven and on earth that converge in unity before the Throne. Corporate intercessory worship is the primary means God uses to release His power. It is the most powerful weapon that exists.

The **House of Prayer in any particular city** is the whole Church in this area (consisting of all the congregations). One particular Day & Night prayer ministry is **NOT** the House of Prayer in a city. It functions with others as a "gas station that squirts gasoline" on the prayer furnace of the Church of that particular city. Ministries with a heightened focus on prayer are only catalysts not the whole House of Prayer.

The eternal identity of the whole Body of Christ is the House of Prayer. This is not just true of ministries that focus on 24/7 prayer. The Father governs the universe in intimate partnership with His people. This is the ultimate expression of His desire for partnership. When we see our destiny as the House of Prayer it gives us resolve with confidence that God will empower us to walk in the grace of prayer. It also shows us the significant loss we incur if we neglect prayer.

We are **called** or named the House of Prayer by God, angels, demons and the saints. When God names a person or nation it indicates their character and how they function in the Holy Spirit. Our greatest place of authority, honor, dignity and security is found in this reality. The Church in the nations does not yet see her identity as being an eternal House of Prayer. As the Lord wrestled with Jacob and changed his name, so He is wrestling with the Body of Christ to change our name (identity) and thus, the way we see ourselves before Him.

> 24 *A Man wrestled with him until the breaking of day...28 He said, "Your name shall no longer be called Jacob, but Israel; you struggled with God and...prevailed." (Gen. 32:24-28)*

Jacob's name means "supplanter" (or manipulator or deceiver). Israel means to "prevail as a prince with God". Our natural mindset without the aid of the Holy Spirit is to think like Jacob. Jesus will not come back until the Church knows who she is and functions in light of it.

> 17 *And the Spirit and the Bride say, "Come!" (Rev. 22:17)*

Jesus comes back at the Second Coming in answer to global concerts of prayer. The End-Time prayer movement in partnership with Jesus' heavenly intercession will release the Great Harvest, the Great Tribulation and even drive Satan "the usurper" off this planet (Rev. 20).

> *10 Sing to the LORD a new song, and His praise from the ends of the earth, you who go down to the sea...you coastlands and you inhabitants of them! 11 Let the wilderness and its cities lift up their voice...13 The Lord shall go forth like a mighty man (Second Coming); He shall stir up His zeal like a man of war...He shall prevail against His enemies. (Is 42:10-13)*

Jesus Created and Continues To Rule by Intercession

The Father oversaw creation by releasing His power as Jesus spoke out His plans before Him. This is the foundational principle of intercession: the Father's thoughts (plans) are spoken by Jesus (intercession) then the Holy Spirit releases power (Gen 1:3, 9, 11, 15, 24, 30).

> *2 The earth was without form, and void...and the Spirit of God was hovering over the face of the waters. 3 Then God (Jesus) said, "Let there be light"; and there was light. (Gen 1:2-3)*

Jesus expressed Himself as an "intercessory oracle" as creator. He manifests His power in the earthly realm by living before the Father with intercessory authority as the "The Word".

> *6 By the word of the LORD the heavens were made, and all the host of them by the breath of His mouth. (Ps. 33:6)*

The majesty of intercession is seen in the fact that Jesus will continue to govern with it.

> *25 Therefore He is also able to save to the uttermost those who come to God through Him, since He always lives to make intercession for them. (Heb. 7:25)*

Jesus creates then upholds or holds together (Col. 1:17) the created order by speaking the Word to the Father in the present tense. This is one form of intercession that Jesus engages in forever.

> *3 (Jesus)...upholding all things by the Word of His power... (Heb. 1:3) 17 He (Jesus) is before all things, and in Him all things consist (hold together: NIV). (Col. 1:17)*

David received revelation of Jesus as the Messianic King using intercession in taking possession of each area of each nation including political, economic, spiritual, educational, military, agricultural, family, media, arts, technology, environment, social institutions, etc. (Ps. 2:7-9).

> *7 The LORD (Father) has said to Me (Jesus)...8 "Ask of Me, and I will give You the nations for Your inheritance, and the ends of the earth for Your possession." (Ps. 2:7-8)*

Jesus rules the nations through intercession now and in the age-to-come. Prayer will not become obsolete in the age-to-come but it will be far more central in our lives. Jesus will rule as a king in context to His high priestly ministry of intercession. One aspect of the order of Melchizedek is to rule through intercession (Gen. 14:18; Heb. 5:6, 10; 6:20; 7:1-28).

> *4 You (Jesus) are a priest forever according to the order of Melchizedek. (Ps. 110:4)*

Solomon prophesied that prayer would be made continually for Jesus in the Millennial Kingdom. The fullness of God dwells in Jesus, so He does not personally need our prayers (Col. 2:9). However, we will pray continually for strength for those in Jesus' governmental administration. The principle of praying for those in authority continues in the age-to-come.

> *15 And He (Jesus in the Millennial Kingdom) shall live; and the gold of Sheba will be given to Him; prayer also will be made for Him continually, and daily He shall be praised. (Ps. 72:15) 1 I exhort that...intercessions...be made 2 for kings and all who in authority... (1 Tim. 2:1-2)*

The Centrality of Intercession in God's Plan

Human history began with daily prayer meetings in the Garden of Eden (Gen. 3:8). Israel began as a nation at a prayer meeting after leaving Egypt (Ex. 19:6-20). At this time, God revealed their "House of Prayer identity" in calling them to rule as priests (prayer/worship, etc).

> *6 You (Israel) shall be to Me a kingdom of priests and a holy nation. (Ex. 19:6) 10 Have made us kings and priests to our God; and we shall reign on the earth. (Rev. 5:10)*

Israel's first building project was to build a Worship Sanctuary or House of Prayer (Ex. 25:2). One of the first things David did after becoming king over Jerusalem was to establish 24/7 worship there (1 Chr. 15-16). David financed 4,000 paid musicians, 288

114

singers and 4,000 gatekeepers (1 Chr. 23:5; 25:7). Thus, about 10,000 full-time staff facilitated worship. It would cost $200 million a year to provide $3,000 a month for 5,000 full-time people (with buildings). David commanded God's people to honor the heavenly order of worship that he received by revelation because it was God's command (2 Chr. 29:25; 35:4, 15; Ezra 3:10; Neh. 12:45). Israel was restored by Daniel's intercession that moved angels and demons (Dan. 10:12). Zerubbabel (about 536 BC) established full-time singers and musicians as commanded by David (Ezra 3:10-11; Neh. 12:47). Ezra and Nehemiah (445 BC) established full-time singers and musicians as David commanded (Neh. 12:24, 45).

Jesus began His public ministry in a prayer meeting in the wilderness (Mt. 4) and ended it in a prayer meeting in the garden of Gethsemane (Mt. 26).The Church began in a prayer meeting (Acts 1-2) and will end natural history in context to a global prayer movement (Rev. 22:17; 5:8; 8:4; Lk. 18:7-8; Mt. 25:1-13; Isa. 62:6-7; 24:14-16; 25:9; 26:8-9; 27:2-5, 13; 30:18-19; 42:10-13; 43:26; 51:11; 52:8; Joel 2:12-17, 32; Jer. 31:7; Amos 9:11-12; Mic. 5:3-4; Zeph. 2:1-3; Ps. 102:17-20; 122:6; Zech. 12:10, etc.). The conflict at the end-of-the-age will be between two Houses of Prayer (two global worship movements). The Holy Spirit is raising up the most powerful worship movement in history to defeat the Antichrist's End-Time worldwide false worship movement.

> *8 All who dwell on the earth will worship him (Antichrist), whose names have not been written in the Book of Life of the Lamb slain from the foundation of the world. (Rev. 13:8)*

Rev. 4-5 describes the worship order around God's Throne. Those nearest God's Throne agree with Him in 24/7 worship and intercession as the most exalted occupation in the New Jerusalem.

8 The 4 living creatures...do not rest day or night, saying: "Holy, holy, holy..." (Rev. 4:8)

Our Ultimate Privilege in God's Grace: Being a House of Prayer

3 Do not let the son of the foreigner who has joined himself to the LORD speak, saying, "The LORD has utterly separated me (making me second class citizen in the Kingdom) from His people"; nor let the eunuch say, "Here I am, a dry tree (I have no future honor because I have no children)." 4 For thus says the LORD: "To the eunuchs who...choose what pleases Me, and hold fast My covenant, 5 Even to them I will give in My House and within My walls a place and a name better than that of sons and daughters (the honor given by the heritage of children); I will give them an everlasting name that shall not be cut off. 6 Also the sons of the foreigner who join themselves to the LORD... to love the name of the Lord...7 Even them I will bring to My holy mountain, and make them joyful in

My House of Prayer...For My House (God's eternal family including His resources) shall be called a House of Prayer for all nations."

8 The Lord GOD, who gathers the outcasts of Israel, says, "Yet I will gather to him others (Gentiles) besides those who are gathered to him (Israel)." (Isa. 56:3-8)

Isaiah explains the greatness of our calling by emphasizing that even the most unlikely outcasts (foreigners and eunuchs) will receive the highest place of honor (Isa. 56:1-8). He had no stronger way to make his point than revealing that the redeemed are forever called the House of Prayer. The foreigner is so transformed and exalted in God's grace that this is their destiny and identity.

A. **Foreigners:** were idolatrous and immoral people who were often demonized

B. **I will bring them:** the Lord will supernaturally help foreigners to develop a prayer life

C. **Eunuchs:** could not have children thus they had no physical heritage to continue their family name. In the ancient world, after a military defeat men were sometimes made eunuchs with the intention that as slaves they would serve in a king's courts, etc.

D. **I will give a place and a name better than:** eunuchs who obey God will be given a place of significance and a name of honor that is better than the significant place and honor that their children could bring them.

E. **Everlasting name:** the faithful will have an everlasting name of honor in the Kingdom

F. **I will make them joyful:** our joy in the Millennial Kingdom will be partially found in functioning in God's family as the House of Prayer that releases God's resource into the nations of the earth. This describes the measure of transformation that will happen to the foreigners.

We must shake off the spirit of passivity. We must remove all that hinders God's Word from moving our heart and thus all that keeps us from speaking God's word back to Him.

> *1 Awake, awake! Put on your strength, O Zion; put on your beautiful garments, O Jerusalem...2 Shake yourself from the dust, arise...O Jerusalem! Loose yourself from the bonds of your neck, O captive daughter of Zion! (Isa. 52:1-2)*

My House shall be Called the House of Prayer

CHAPTER 8

PRAYING CHURCH PRINCIPLE #5 - People in the House - *Racial Reconciliation*

> **Mar 11:17** *And he taught, saying unto them, Is it not written, My house shall be **called of all nations** the house of prayer?.*

> **Isa 2:2** *And it shall come to pass in the last days, that the mountain of the LORD'S house shall be established in the top of the mountains, and shall be exalted above the hills; AND ALL NATIONS SHALL FLOW UNTO IT.*

In the last days *ALL NATIONS* will be summonsed, called and flow into the house of the Lord established in the top of the mountain, representing the place of prayer. Therefore, the re-establishing of the house of prayer identity of the church and the inclusion of all nationalities, ethnicities and people groups being represented in His house of prayer are one in the same movements in the end-time church. If God's house is to be revived and once again known as a house of prayer it's going to have to include all nations. Today, because the church, both African-American and Caucasian in America, has cultivated a culture of prayerlessness and have turned to merchandising, worldly business practices and the arm of the flesh in building and running our churches, we have cultivated a culture of segregation, separation, pervasive racism, division and disunity within the body of Christ. All nations will only be represented within the context of a praying people that have laid their lives down, taken up their cross, and have followed Jesus into the full manifestation of the one new man in the earth – The Church.

119

My House shall be Called the House of Prayer

In November 2011 at the 24hr Call Prayer meeting in Detroit Michigan, during one of the prayer sets there was a time of prayer for the reconciliation of the blacks and whites in our nation. It was a very intense time, as a noted African-American Bishop in Detroit recounted the history of racism in America, with Slavery, share-cropping and Jim Crow laws, and in Detroit, with industrial share cropping with the Ford Motor Company and Henry Ford. At the end of this time of retrospection of America's unfortunate history of racism and discrimination this African-American Bishop turned to the white ministers on the platform and said, "My father, *who is 96 years old, told me to forgive white people for what they did to our forefathers, and if I would forgive without anyone apologizing, he said one day a white person would apologize to me for what white people have done to our forefathers.* " He then turned to the white ministers on the platform and said, *"So now I want you to apologize to me."*

At that time many of the white ministers began to graciously oblige his request by apologizing and asking for forgiveness on behalf of what their forefathers did to our forefathers. After this, a young African-American minister on the platform felt the need to also apologize to the white ministers on the platform for what African-Americans have held against white people for what they had done to our forefathers. He referred to it as "REVERSE RACISM," saying he struggled with marrying his wife, who happened to be white, because of how he felt his family and friends would think about him marrying a white woman. He stated that many African-Americans struggled with these feelings about marrying outside of their race because of how they will be perceived, both by African-American women, and by bitter, unforgiving African-Americans in general.

He also went on to state that many African-Americans that voted for President Barak Obama just because he was Black operated in the same spirit of White prejudice and racism that has been perpetuated upon African-Americans for years. When he asked if all the African-American ministers could come together for a time of reconciliation, to apologize to our white brethren and pray for this counter thought pattern of prejudice, bitterness and reverse racism to be broken over our people, he was resisted by an older African-American Bishop, also from the city of Detroit. This Bishop stated that African-Americans should not have to apologize for any counter feelings of prejudice, bitterness or so-called "Reverse Racism, because we are the ones that have been unjustly treated, and we've never received a formal apology. And no doubt, he said, her family probably didn't want her to marry you, as much as your family had reservations about you marrying her.

To say the least, this was a very intense time between these two people groups represented, being played out before 40,000 people on the stage at Ford Field in Detroit, and before millions by way of satellite T.V. and the live web-stream. At this time and in this setting I was asked to share my testimony of deliverance from these same feelings of prejudice, bitterness and reverse racism that took place 20 years prior in my life. The next two chapters of this book are dedicated to what I shared at this Call Prayer gathering in Detroit, as well as what I believe is the root of all racism.

Racisms Religious Roots

I began sharing by stating that racism did not begin with Slavery, the Share-cropping system, or Jim Crow laws. Racism began with religion. One of the greatest blights on the First Century Church is the initial racial divide that occurred as the Gentile community of believers outgrew the Jewish community of believers and began separating from them and persecuting them as early as the 3rd century. This racism had profound implications for the church. This separation is felt to this day in Jewish distrust of the very people that carry their own Scriptures. If we're ever going to reverse the curse of racism in the earth we're going to have to begin, not with the legal system or by recounting all that has happened to African-Americans over the last 400 years of slavery and discrimination, and demanding an apology for these atrocities, No! We're going to have to go to the root of racism, and repent for the foundation that enabled a system of racism to exist.

Jesus Takes a Stand against Racism

One of the strongest statements against racism in the body of Christ was uttered by Jesus Christ. It's actually the statement Jesus made in Mark 11:17, quoting from Isaiah 56:7, about the inclusion of all races in his house of prayer. Jesus said, "My house shall be called of all nations the house prayer." Jesus did not just state this in His vehement anger only because of the corruption of the merchandising of animal sacrifices alone, which was going on in the temple. Jesus was not only upset because of this buying and selling that was taking place in the temple, but I believe he was also just as upset because of where in the temple it was taking place. They were using the courts of the Gentiles to buy and sell animal sacrifices for the Holy days. The courts of the Gentiles were where the Gentiles were allowed to come and pray. This area was now being used by the Jewish religious leaders for unjust monetary gain for the temple, probably out of their disdain and racists attitudes for the Gentiles. In this religious community and place of worship racists' attitudes was actually interfering with the Gentiles coming to the house of prayer.

The premier verse displaying Jesus' righteous indignation was displayed against racism in the house of God. We often quote the first part of his statement, "My house shall be called a house of prayer," but forget or overlook the latter part of that verse which says, *FOR* ALL NATIONS. This part of Jesus' statement reveals the purpose of God's house, as well as God's chosen nation, Israel – to be a light to the Gentiles. This phrase *"For all Nations"* is as important as the first part of this statement made by Jesus, because it reveals what was actually the focus of His displeasure. The Gentile nations were being discriminated against and inhibited from coming to God's house, keeping God's house from the power of its purpose — *PRAYER FOR ALL NATIONS TO BE RECONCILED TO GOD.* Thusly God's house was not fulfilling its purpose as a House of Prayer *FOR ALL NATIONS.*

Sunday Mornings: Still the Most Segregated Hour of the Week.

In the 1960's civil rights movement, in the midst of the struggle for desegregation in American society, Dr. Martin Luther King Jr. famously declared that "11 o'clock on Sunday morning is the most segregated hour of the week." Sadly, this still holds true, even today, 50 years after the desegregation of public facilities in America. In the church which has lost its purpose and has cultivated a culture of prayerlessness, we still have a racially segregated Church in America, keeping the church from her purpose as a place of prayer for all nations. What's even sadder for African-American Christians and unbelievers alike is that though the walls of segregation were removed by the sacrifice of our forefathers in the civil rights movement who gave their lives to assure that we would have some of the civil liberties and privileges we have today, the church in this generation still gravitates to our segregated houses of worship. Our forefathers sacrificed being ridiculed, terrorized, homes and churches bombed, beaten, and some even killed, so that the walls of partition and separation keeping racial groups divided would be torn down in this nation, and so that we could be integrated into American society.

Yet, in many circles of society today African-Americans still acclimate to our segregated public accommodations. No place is this acclimation to segregation in the public square seen more than in our segregated Churches. Our Churches are still the most segregated hour of the week. Our Church leaders still operate and run our churches by a bankrupt religious system that keeps our churches doctrinally and racially segregated, and many of our attendees and members still prefer these segregated churches. Though some of this is due to some systemic and economic demographics still at work in our society that keeps our neighborhoods segregated, by in large, we are still segregated in our churches because of either, the fear of stepping out of our racial comfort zones, religious tradition and control, or cultural worship preferences that we are unwilling to let go of. And in some cases we're still segregated within our churches because our church leaders still struggle with bitterness, and un-forgiveness that they are unwilling to let go of to assure that integration within the body of Christ is the norm in the church, and not the exception. These and many other similar dynamics, keep African-Americans, as well as other racial groups, segregated within the body of Christ.

Our Houses of worship, with their religious spirits, along with our cultural preferences, fear and pent up un-forgiveness, do more to continue to keep us divided along racial lines than any other sociological dynamic today. Racism in modern civilization did not start with Slavery or Jim Crow laws. It began with Religion, so it can't be totally done away with through governmental legislation. Racism in modern civilization, because it has its roots beginning in a House of Worship, between Jew and Gentile, must be dealt with through the spiritual weapons of prayer that produces a revelation of Jesus Christ. Societal desegregation through legislation was meant to deal with our laws that were keeping the races divided, but for us to be united and reconciled to one another our religion must deal with our hearts that keep the races divided.

My House shall be Called the House of Prayer

I believe God wants to raise up forerunners at the end of the age, that take the message of reconciliation, fullness and the coming of the Lord to the nations of the world. I believe that just as during the era of the Civil Rights movement African-Americans in American society must take the lead in this charge towards true reconciliation of all races in God's house. I believe we have a debt to pay to our forefathers and a responsibility to them to continue the fight for integration and reconciliation in our hearts in this generation, to make what they endured in their lives in their generation lasting and meaningful. Especially in the church of America, the one place where we should be integrated, Christians have a responsibility to come together across racial and ethnic lines to integrate and be reconciled, not only for the sake of past generations of freedom fighters, but for Jesus Christ, who died, was buried and rose again so that we would be one in Christ.

However, today, just like in Jesus' time when he visited the temple, and just like right before the civil rights movement, we have turned from a culture of prayer in our churches that brings together all races in Christ, to religion and the spirit of culturalism. We have turned to merchandising, corporate structuring, and entertainment in building the church of Jesus Christ, producing a culture of performance, competition and religious bigotry that further exacerbates the racial divide in the church. Therefore our churches are not being run by a dependency upon God in prayer, but primarily by manipulation and control through the spirit of performance. All of this, in addition to an elitist approach of relating in the church from the Clergy to the laity produces the same spirit of control behind racism that was at work during Slavery and Colonialism in the middle ages to control Africans on the plantations of their masters.

This spirit of control behind racism, which is the spirit of superiority and domination of one people group over another, is actually what fuels the present system of religious, clergy hierarchy operating in the church today. This is actually what promotes and empowers the clergy and laity divisions and distinctions, which results in religious and ministerial bigotry, with our churches now becoming the Plantations, our Pastors are our *Massa*, and his, "so called" members, the slaves for his vision. This spirit and system is one of the things which lead to pervasive racism within the body of Christ. This is what divides and isolates churches, ministry gifts and people groups within the body of Christ. This way of relating between the clergy and the laity within the Church of Jesus Christ was not seen when Jesus interacted with his disciples or with the common people he ministered to while on the earth in the first century church. It was seen however, in how the Pharisees and religious leaders related with the common people during this same period of time. This is a religious and controlling spirit behind racism and bigotry in the church. This is the spirit that produces the superiority and domination in the church in how Pastors and Church leaders relate within their congregations. This is the religious spirit behind racism that must be broken for the body of Christ to come together in his house of prayer.

Coming Out Of My Racial, Religious, and Cultural Comfort Zones

Having grown up in the church I know firsthand how you can be a Christian whose faith has at the center of its worship a Jewish man who is from another ethnicity of 97% of his followers, and still struggle with racial and religious bigotry and prejudice. I know how as a Christian you can still be struggling with bitter feelings of un-forgiveness against other races, while claiming to worship a man who died on the cross for our sins, saying, *"Father forgive them, for they know not what they do."* This was my experience growing up in my African-American Church expression of Christianity. This is my story of how I was set free from religious and racial bigotry, bitterness, un-forgiveness and fear, and didn't even know I was bound.

As an African-American my experience with bitterness and un-forgiveness against other races, was actually cultivated within my religious, African-American church experience. My sour racial mindsets stemmed from the fact that in our church setting we did not associate or interact with other races, even though in society the races had been desegregated for over 40 years. I really cannot recall a single negative experience with any other ethnicity that could contribute to why I did not want to associate with other races or harbored racists' views and thought patterns towards other races. When I was born the civil rights movement had already removed the legislated barriers of racial discrimination and segregation with the desegregation of all public facilities in the 1960's. But in our churches and communities we were still segregated. Within our church upbringing, there was a culture of distain and bitterness towards what was done to my ancestors, which was a part of our church culture. We were always talking about what Caucasians were doing to hold us back, or what they had done to us in the past.

This caused me to withdraw from Caucasian people, and Caucasian churches, thusly developing in me a reactionary prejudiced attitude towards Caucasians. Not having fostered relationships with people of other ethnicities, I built my racial world view exclusively on my association with preachers and teachers who were bitter and offended from their experiences, or their parents and grandparents experiences with Caucasian people. So I grew up dealing with racist and prejudicial thought patterns towards Caucasians because I had never been outside of my racial culture to experience relationships with other ethnicities. I did not have any positive experiences to empower me to see Caucasian people the way God saw them. Our church bred in us an "us against them" mentality, in how we worshipped, how we preached, how we prayed, how we looked at life and how we voted politically. This kept us exclusive and secluded from the moving of God's spirit within the universal body of Christ.

This is where I'm sending you

This all began to change when my father started his own church in 1987 when I was 21 years old. I remember the first time I was challenged to come out of my familiar cultural surroundings. I was in my second year of ministry and desiring to go to Bible College. I had been praying about where God wanted me to go. One day I went to the mail box to get the mail at my parents' house and retrieved a magazine sent to my baby sister, who was 12 years old. The magazine was from a ministry on the outskirts of town that I had never heard of. On the front of the magazine it had the pastor in a preaching pose, and 7 characteristics of the church of the 90's. It was 1990 and the magazine intrigued me because I had just finished a message on the church of the 1990s and the coming glory of this decade. Everything that God had given me to preach was in the magazine article. On the back it had 10 reasons why you should come to this church's Bible institute. I heard the spirit of God speak up in my spirit and say, "THIS IS WHERE I'M SENDING YOU TO BIBLE COLLEGE."

Immediately I began to make excuses for why I could not go to this Bible College. It was not an accredited institution and I was almost finished with College courses at an accredited State College in my City. Our church did not believe the same way concerning baptism, which was a major stronghold in the denomination I had grown up in. We were Oneness Apostolic. We worshipped one way and they worshipped another way. Our church was small and there's a mega church. But what I was afraid of most of all was that our church was African American and theirs was Caucasian/Anglo-Saxon, and I had never been outside of my race for any type of church or religious experience.

Obeying the Leading of the Lord

I thought that I had a way out of going to this school. My father was my pastor and I thought that he would never let me go to that church because of the differing beliefs. Doctrinally, we were staunchly against Trinitarianism, (which we thought was the teaching of the belief in three gods), and against anyone that didn't baptize in Jesus name. We didn't fellowship with anyone who didn't believe the same as us in these areas. So when I went to my father and told him what God was speaking to me, I thought he would say, "We don't believe the same, so I would advise against it." Instead he said, "If God is dealing with you about going to school out there, you need to obey the leading of the Lord."

Well, to say the least I was very nervous about this step out of my comfort zone, but I obeyed the Lord and enrolled in this Bible College. I was one of about 10 African-Americans in the student body of about 500 students. However, through the spirit of God I began to feel increasingly comfortable in this new setting and surrounding I was placed in. I began to develop friendships with those of other races, denominations, and cultures. I soon realized that I was missing a proper understanding of other cultures, teachings and ethnic expressions of worship. My heart began to be knitted to the Lord's heart concerning other nations, races and other aspects of Christ's nature.

I begin to know the Lord in a way I had never known him before. My relationship with the Lord increased what seemed like 10-fold. I began receiving revelation from the Lord concerning His mission and calling for the nations of the world. I began to desire to pray and seek His face as I never had before. As a result of seeking the

Lord in this manner, I began to realize that every ethnicity, people group, and denomination is a unique part of Christ. I understood that we won't see the body of Christ functioning fully, until we come together in unity. I also learned that each ethnicity, denomination, and culture is a piece of the puzzle and a key that unlocks our own individual and corporate destinies in Christ. We were created to need one another to fulfill what God has called us to do and to be.

I was delivered from, fear, bitterness, and prejudice, just by being in the midst of another ethnic expression and developing heart relationships with these people. I learned what the Love of God is and what it is for, as I saw John 3:16 through the lens of the whole world, not just my little part of the world. John 3:16 says, "**God**, so Loved, the **world**..." (Polar opposites, God and the world, brought together by love)... "**That He gave His only begotten Son**." I learned and saw firsthand in this multi-ethnic setting that the love of God is for OPPOSITES. It's for someone that is not like you. It is for someone that has not treated you the way you might have wanted to be treated. It is for those that don't look, act, think or live like you. When you learn to love those who are different from you and even those who mistreat you, you are walking in the love of God. When this happens, not only do you get what you have, but you get what they have. You become a new man, enabling you to accomplish more for God, more for others, and more for yourself.

As I came into a diverse community of believers in that Bible College over twenty years ago, I began to receive a new heart, and when I did, I became a new man. I soon realized, as God began to open my understanding about His end-time purpose for the nations coming together in His house of prayer that I was sent as a forerunner into this ministry. I was called to help prepare this church in my city to enter into reconciliation and the fullness of its calling. As I was given opportunities to grow in this ministry through serving, loving and speaking in this church's Bible College, I began to see my place in this community of believers. Over a period of ten years, spanning from the end of the twentieth century to the beginning of the twenty-first century, the racial landscape of this international mega-church in Columbus Ohio went from 5% African-American to 55% African-American.

Consequently, I came on staff at this church as its first African-American pulpit staff minister. The Caucasians and African-Americans within this ministry were completely integrated, thus positioning them to be reconciled to one another. This ministry became one of the foremost Christian ministries on the earth during that period. The scope of this ministry's reach went from a local outreach influence to a national and international reach, influencing this nation and the nations of the world. I watched this ministry's influence and affect in the world increase seemingly a hundredfold, as it embraced the nations and ethnic groups of the world. I believe I was sent into this ministry as a forerunner to be a part of the establishing of God's house of prayer for all nations. I was sent to help prepare this ministry to be a forerunner and a prototype of what was coming in the twenty-first century; preparing His people for the coming of the Lord.

My House shall be Called the House of Prayer

CHAPTER 9

PRAYING CHURCH PRINCIPLE #5 *Continued* - The Making of a New Race

In order for the body of Christ to come to the fullness of power to fulfill our calling and purpose in the earth we must come to the unity of the faith, unto a perfect or mature man. The Church was meant to be the place that united all nations into the unity of the faith of Jesus Christ. How does the church come into the unity of all nations to make them joyful in His house of prayer? In order for the church to come to this type of unity we must truly become the Church of God in Christ. Not the African- American denomination which is the largest African-American denomination in the world (*COGIC- Church of God in Christ*), but the Church of God must truly get in Christ.

The Church which is in Christ is actually a new race of people. 2 Corinthians 5:17 says, *Therefore if <u>any man be in Christ</u>, he is a new creature.* When we are born again into the family of God and begin attending the church of God, we are coming, not to have church, not to have a good time, nor just to fellowship, but to become a new creation in Christ, a new race of people, complete with our particular distinctions and ethnic diversities and individualities within His body, the church. We are actually coming to be perfected in one, in order that we might be placed and positioned to fulfill our membership ministries and our national callings in the earth. Paul explained it like this in Ephesians 4:11-13

> *And he gave some, apostles; and some, prophets; and some, evangelists; and some, pastors and teachers; For the perfecting of the saints, for the*

work of the ministry, for the edifying of the body of Christ: <u>*Till, we all come to the unity of the faith, and of the knowledge of the Son of God, unto a perfect man, unto the measure of the stature of the fullness of Christ.*</u>

The Origin of the Nations is the Key to Reuniting the Nations

How do the nations with ethnic diversities, and cultural distinctions and particular and different strengths, weaknesses and purposes come into unity within one body? We must understand the position we are called to fulfill within the body of Christ. Furthermore, we must understand that our individual and national destinies - *where we're going, and what we're called to do as a people in the earth*, is connected in some degree to our heritage in the earth - *where we've come from in the earth*. God always deals in geographic regions when dealing with people. People and their prophetic destinies and promises in scripture are always tied to a geographic region or plot of land. As many different people groups coming together in one body there are 3 main things we must come to understand if we're going to come together and realize our individual, corporate and national destinies in Christ. When we do, we will realize our significance as a people, recognizing our need for one another and coming together into fullness. The 3 things we must understand are:

1. Where we've come from as a people, both in heaven and the earth, *not just heaven*.
2. We must know where our story and plight is in scripture.
3. In understanding the origin of all people groups, we must understand that in the formation of the nations all people groups were originally created to be in unity in the earth.

The Origin of the Nations

To understand this origin of unity within the nations Acts 17:26 gives us a launching pad to explain how the nations were all made from one blood. We further see after the formation of the nations, how we were all separated at the tower of Babel. In that separation we've all gone on to have a separate place of habitation in the earth where we've developed our own individualities, our own culture and our own distinct physical features based on our geographical proximity to the sun. In that separation we've all had an appointed time of leadership in the earth where we developed and excelled over and above the other, instead of together and with the other in mind. In this appointed time we've all attempted to find God separated from each other. However, in our reconciliation we will all truly find God and the fullness of who we are by coming together in one body again to love God, and one another, even as we love ourselves and how God made us.

> *Acts 17:26 And he hath made of one blood all nations of men for to dwell on all the face of the earth, and hath determined the times before appointed, and the bounds of their habitation; Acts 17:27 That they should seek the Lord, if haply they might feel after him, and find him, though he be not far from every one of us: Act 17:28 For in him we live, and move, and have our being; as certain also of your own poets have said, For we are also his offspring.*

These verses in Acts 17:26-28 say a lot. Firstly it says He hath made of one blood *ALL* nations. Secondly it says, *ALL* nations were made to dwell on *ALL* the face of the earth. Next it says He hath determined an appointed time of leadership in the earth for the nations. (*I believe to develop their individual leadership traits*).

135

Next it says, there would be boundaries given for these nations to live within (*I believe to form their individual identities and features*). Next it says, these nations would seek after God within these boundaries, but they would not find him fully until *THEY CAME TOGETHER* to live, move and have their being in HIM. And lastly it says, we are ALL from Him, (*his offspring*) born and made with certain individualities as an expression of His diversity. This scripture depicts for us the ultimate purpose and destiny of the scattering and uniting of the nations in the beginning formation of the races, and at the end of the age. It depicts the purposes of our boundaries that were given and the goal of our scattering over the expanse of the earth, with the eventual results of our coming together at the end of the age- *that we would find the fullness of God in and through one another.*

What Blood do all Nations come from

Acts 17:26 says, All nations come from one blood. Who is the one blood that all nations have come from? The one blood that all nations come from is found in the table of the nations in Genesis Ch. 10.

> *1 Now these are the generations of the sons of Noah, Shem, Ham, and Japheth: and unto them were sons born after the flood. Gen 10:5 By these were the isles of the Gentiles divided in their lands; every one after his tongue, after their families, IN THEIR NATIONS.*

It is from one blood, the blood of Noah, that all nations were made. Noah's three sons were the foundation for the new world after the flood. In Genesis 9 the bible says, that Noah and his three sons were blessed and told to be fruitful and multiply and replenish the earth. The three sons of Noah were Ham, Shem and Japheth. *FROM THESE THREE SONS ALL NATIONS HAVE ORIGINATED.*

136

Dominion is based on Communion and Relational Connectedness

The three sons of Noah were mandated to be fruitful and multiply and replenish the earth, and have dominion.   This was God's original command to Adam in the beginning. But because Adam did not stay connected with God in heaven because of sin, he was unable to accomplish this mandate.   He was fruitful and he multiplied, those two commands required his connection to the earth. However, Adam having dominion and subduing the earth required righteousness – right standing with God and man.   The dominion in the earth of man is directly connected to man's ability to be together in unity with God who created the earth and man whom he gave individual purpose in the earth. Without a relational connection with the God of heaven and earth, and with individual persons that God put in the earth to corporately bring about the purpose for the earth, mankind is unable to have dominion and subdue the earth.   Thusly, these two failures led to the destruction of all men in the earth.   However, Noah was spared the judgment of the flood because he was righteous in an unrighteous world.

> *Gen 7:1 And the LORD said unto Noah, Come thou and all thy house into the ark; for thee have I seen righteous before me in this generation.*

If the three sons of Noah were going to be able to accomplish the mandate of God to have dominion they were going to have to stay together in unity and intimacy with God and one another. God created the 3 sons in the earth to be in unity so as to rule and reign in the earth as the God-head ruled in heaven. As God is a triune God, Father, Son and Holy Ghost ruling the heavens as One God, so mankind was created to rule and reign in the earth as a triune people from the three sons of Noah, Ham, Shem, and Japheth. We will prove this from scripture later in this chapter.

137

The dominion of Noah's three sons was going to be based on their communion, or relational connectedness (unity with God & Man). They were to go forth with the vision of God for the earth, not their own individual visions. They were to go forth to prepare the earth for God to enter it with His righteous seed to produce righteous fruit in the earth. As God in heaven is Father, Son and Holy Ghost - One God, they were to be in the earth, Shem, Ham and Japheth - One man. But because of their unrighteous nature, they were unable to stay in unity with God or one another to accomplish his vision and purpose for the earth. Therefore, they were unable to subdue the earth in preparation to have dominion in the earth. Again, our dominion in the earth is contingent upon our continued relational connectedness with God and with one another. However, there can be no communion, no oneness, no relational connectedness, or unity without an understanding of purpose amongst the subjects involved.

Understanding of Purpose Dispels Strife

Understanding of individual purpose dispels strife. Understanding of national purpose dispels competition and wars. Nations were not created to be like one another. People, families, and countries were not created to be like one another. Nations were created to be themselves and do what God created them to do, together with the other doing what God created the other to do, coming together to fulfill the total plan of the earth through mankind in right relationship with God and one another. Instead of ruling and reigning together in unity they went forth separately at different intervals of times in the earth in the 6000 years of man's lease on the earth to attempt to have dominion, ruling and reigning apart from the other. At the same time they attempted to hold the other down, when they should have been working together to subdue the earth for the purpose of preparing the earth for God's presence to return.

The Times Before Appointed

In the year 2000 the earth became approximately 6000 years old. Man was created on the 6th day to subdue and have dominion in the earth to prepare the earth for heaven to inhabit it. When Adam sinned he surrendered his authority in the earth to Satan, and Satan went about preparing the earth for his habitation. For thousands of years Satan has been attempting to exercise his authority with this lease he received from man, trying to establish his kingdom in the earth. The purpose of the Church is to receive back this authority Jesus took from Satan at Calvary, to take back the lease and bind Satan and His kingdom and loose the kingdom of God in the earth.

> *Mat 16:18 And I say also unto thee, that thou art Peter, and upon this rock I will build my church; and the gates of hell shall not prevail against it. 19 And I will give unto thee the keys of the kingdom of heaven: and whatsoever thou shalt bind on earth shall be bound in heaven: and whatsoever thou shalt loose on earth shall be loosed in heaven.*

Jesus regained the right and authority to the title deed of the earth on the cross, and gave its keys back to man in the church. In other words, for man to receive authority back in the earth to subdue it for God's coming habitation he's going to have to be in Christ. All three sons from which all nations come from would have to be reconciled in one - *Christ Jesus* - in order for man to take back the earth to offer it up to God for His throne to be established in it.

In the days and years to come, as we go further into the 21st century we're going to see this lease of authority on the earth fully restored back to man, as together with his Church, Jesus takes the scroll during the unique dynamics of the end-times to judge the earth and establish his righteous kingdom in the earth. Only a mature united church can be positioned with Christ to repossess the earth for the Lord and fill it with his glory. This will began the day of Christ and His Church's reign in the earth.

A Day with the Lord is as a Thousand Years

The 6000 years of the earth from Adam's Creation can be equated with the six days of creation in Genesis 1 and 2.

> *Gen 1:31 And God saw everything that he had made, and behold, it was very good. And the evening and the morning were the sixth day.*
> *2 Peter 3:8 says, But, beloved, be not ignorant of this one thing, that a day is with the Lord as a thousand years, and a thousand years as one day.*

The 6th day is the day of mans' creation maturity. The 6 thousand years is the time of the earth's creation maturity, where mankind's time of developing a heart and mind after God will come to its perfection and he will be prepared to host the presence of the God in the earth. This is what Romans 8 speaks of when it says, the earth, all of creation is groaning waiting for the manifestation of the Sons of God. The Earth knows that it's not in its rightful possessors hands, and it's groaning (shaking) to be possessed by the sons of God. It is during this time, when man repossesses the earth at the coming of Christ, that God will establish His millennial reign in the earth with Jesus ruling and reigning through his united Church in the earth. This will begin the day of rest in the earth, the 7th day. The 7th day is the day of God, and of restoration.

> *Gen 2:1 Thus the heavens and the earth were finished, and all the host of them. 2 And on the seventh day God ended his work which he had made; and he rested on the seventh day from all his work which he had made.*

I believe that in the year 2000A.D, we entered the beginnings of the 7th day. From the time of Adam to the time of Abraham is approximately 2000 years. From Abraham to Jesus Christ is approximately 2000 years, and from Jesus Christ to the 21st century is approximately 2000 years, totaling approximately 6000 years of mankind in the earth. All three of the Sons of Noah have had approximately a 2000 year span of time when nations from one of the three sons ruled and reigned in the earth over the nations from the other two sons, a time appointed by God to find and seek after God.

> *Act 17:26 and hath made of one blood all nations of men for to dwell on all the face of the earth, AND HATH DETERMINED THE TIMES BEFORE APPOINTED, AND THE BOUNDS OF THEIR HABITATION: 27. THAT THEY SHOULD SEEK THE LORD, IF HAPLY THEY MIGHT FEEL AFTER HIM, AND FIND HIM, THOUGH HE BE NOT FAR FROM EVERY ONE OF US: 28 for in him we live, and move, and have our being; as certain also of your own poets have said, For we are also his offspring.*

I believe that since the year 2000, the beginning of the 21st century, humanity has been in a state of preparation and positioning, being prepared and positioned to enter the great and terrible day of the Lord, which will culminate in the transition of the earth to the day of rest, known as the millennial reign. In the church we are not only preparing to enter the 7th day as we've gone from the 6 day to the 7th on God's calendar, but we are entering the 3rd day of Resurrection from Pentecost, as we go from the two thousand years from Pentecost into the 3rd thousandth year of the church's existence in the earth from Jesus' ascension. Hosea 6:1-3 says *after two days will he revive us: in the third day he will raise us up, and we shall live in his sight.*

This will represent the time where man is completely restored to the unity it lost at the tower of Babel. God scattered the nations through the scattering of their tongues, as Nimrod, the son of Cush, the son of Ham, attempted to build a tower to heaven to make a name for himself. However, God, on the day of Pentecost released His spirit on the Church to birth His Church and begin the time of the restoration of all things, where all nations would return to unity with God and man, and the earth would be prepared for God to inhabit her once again. As a result of the birthing of the Church on the day of Pentecost, as God poured out his spirit upon all flesh the sons of Noah, Ham, Shem and Japheth will begin to flow back into the House of Prayer as the body of Christ begins to arise and shine to be the light of the nation's leading the nations back to her original purpose in God's body as a House of Prayer for All Nations. How will this flow take place? What will be the process that leads the nations from Noah back into unity in Gods' house of Prayer? How will we come to the place of fullness - *reconciliation, healing and unity for the release of unprecedented power in God's house of prayer*? Let's continue on to see how God has been shaping history to accomplish his purposes for His house of prayer in the earth.

The 3 separate two Thousand Year Reigns of Each Son of Noah in the Earth in History

Within the six days, or six thousand years of man's perfection and maturing in the earth, mankind has been being prepared to rule and reign in the earth in unity. Each nationality from Noah's three sons have exercised a two-thousand year period in which they would attempt to be in authority in the earth, while holding the other two under their domination. During this time they would come to the realization that apart from one another mankind is incapable and unable to accomplish the calling of God for having dominion in the earth. We were made, both as individuals in the beginning and at the formation of the nations, to need God and one another to live and have our being. The latter verse from Acts 17:26 that speaks of God making from one blood all nations, ends in Acts 17:28; saying, *for in him we live, and move, and have our being; as certain also of your own poets have said, for we are also his offspring.*

In these verses describing the formation and arranging of the nations it ends with an interesting acknowledgement. It states, *"For in Him WE live, and move and have our being,"* not I, or they. In order for the nations to live and accomplish their individual callings and responsibilities they must come together in HIM (Christ) to live, move and have their being. The word *"being"* in the original Greek text of the bible, means to exist, it means *"WE ARE."* Each Son of Noah has attempted to rule and reign irrespective of the other, and each one has failed in that period and time frame.

It is it very important for this study for it to be established and continually reiterated that the three sons of Noah - Ham, Shem and Japheth have each had a two-thousand year reign in which they held down their other two brothers while attempting to have dominion in the earth. The order and position of their individual rule in the earth began with Ham, from which the nations listed below established the first great civilizations in the earth – *Egypt, Babylon, Ethiopia,* etc. After Ham's attempt to reign, rule and have dominion in the earth failed, the baton was passed to Shem when Melchizedek blessed and released the promise of the land of Canaan to Abraham in Genesis 14:18

> *Gen 14:18 And Melchizedek king of Salem brought forth bread and wine: and he was the priest of the most high God. 19 And he blessed him, and said, Blessed be Abram of the most high God, possessor of heaven and earth:*

Shem, through Abraham, Isaac, and Jacob, and the Kings of Israel attempted to reign, rule and have dominion the 2nd two-thousand years. And though during the second two-thousand years the seed of God was birth through Jesus Christ being born as the seed of Abraham, seed David, this attempt also failed, as Jesus the seed that would crush the head of the serpent, came to his own and his own received him not. (John 1:12) So from Shem the baton was passed onto Japheth, in the book of Acts, as Peter was summoned by the Roman Centurion Cornelius, to speak unto him the words of life in Acts 10, and as Paul, the Apostle of Jesus Christ declared His intention and call to the be a light to the Gentiles. It was here that the European nations of the Japhetic line would begin the preaching and spreading of the gospel in the 3rd two-thousand year period.

> *Peter unlocks the door to the Gentiles to receive the message and mantle for the spreading of the gospel in Acts 10:1*

> *Acts 10:1 There was a certain man in Caesarea called Cornelius, a centurion of the band called the Italian band, 2 A devout man, and one that feared God with all his house, which gave much alms to the people, and prayed to God always. 3 He saw in a vision evidently about the ninth hour of the day an angel of God coming in to him, and saying unto him, Cornelius. 4 And when he looked on him, he was afraid, and said, what is it, Lord? And he said unto him, Thy prayers and thine alms are come up for a memorial before God. 5 And now send men to*

144

> *Joppa, and call for one Simon, whose surname is Peter: 6 He lodges with one Simon a tanner, whose house is by the sea side: he shall tell thee what thou oughtest to do.*

Paul's Call to the Gentiles in Acts 13:46-48

> *Then Paul and Barnabas waxed bold, and said, It was necessary that the word of God should first have been spoken to you: but seeing ye put it from you, and judge yourselves unworthy of everlasting life, lo, we turn to the Gentiles. 47 For so hath the Lord commanded us, saying, I have set thee to be a light of the Gentiles, that thou shouldest be for salvation unto the ends of the earth. 48 And when the Gentiles heard this, they were glad, and glorified the word of the Lord: and as many as were ordained to eternal life believed.*

Once this release and baton handoff was made the Japhethic - *European nations* went forth to rule and reign and attempt to take dominion in the earth. And even though the Roman Empire and many other European dynasties went forth to conquer and overrun the nations from Ham and Shem in the 3rd two-thousand years, they also carried the mantle and message of the gospel in this 3rd two-thousand year period, keeping the light of the message of salvation through Jesus Christ shining to be given to the ends of the earth. Each son from Noah has taking turns attempting to overthrow, overtake and oppress the other two sons, to have dominion in the earth. The order of their dominion began as follows:

1. **Ham -1st 2000 year reign** – Nations from Babylon, Ethiopia, Egypt, Canaan (By-in-large Africans) are the first great civilizations in the earth . Beginning with Nimrod building the tower of Babel the descendents from Ham begins the reign of the first two-thousand years of the nations from the sons of Noah in the earth. (Genesis 2:11-13; 10:1-8).

2. **Shem – 2nd 2000 year reign** - the Middle-eastern nations of the Mesopotamia area of Shem's descendents from Abraham (Jews, Arabs and some Asians) reigned the second two-thousand years, with the possessing of the promised land (of Canaan) and the reign of the Kings of Israel. *(Genesis 14:18-20; Melchizidek baton hand-off from Hametic/Canaanites to Abraham of the Semitic descent for the possessing of the promise land.)*

3. **Japheth – 3rd 2000 year reign** – Western, European and some of Asiatic descent have reigned for the third two-thousand years from Christ to the 21st century, beginning with the coming of the great Roman Empire and the Destruction of Jerusalem in 70AD. *(Acts 13:46-49, Christ, and Paul baton hand-off to gentile believers from Semitic descent to the Gentiles of Japhetic, European descent).*

All of the nations of the world come from one of these three sons of Noah. (Acts 17:26-30) Below is a list of the Table of Nations with the origin of each nation.

Ancestry	Nation	Notes

Japhethic Line:

Japheth	Greeks	*Became known as Gentiles*
(Europe)		
Gomer	Russians	
Britons	Britains	
Magog	Scythians	
Madai	Medes	
Javan	Greeks	
Tubal	Iberians	
Meshech	Muscovites	
Tiras	Thracians	
Ashjenaz	Germans	
Togarmah	Armenians, Turks	
Elisha	Hellenists	All of Greece
Tarshish	Spanish	
Kittim	Cyprus	

Hametic Line:

Cush	Ethiopia	
Mezraim	Egyptian	
Put (Phut or Punt)	Libya	
Canaan	Canaanites	*Only one of*
Ham's sons w/o a homeland		
Seba	Sudan (Sabeans)	
Heth	Hittites	
Ham	American Indian Mongoloids	

Semetic Line:

Shem	Jews	Genesis 10:21
Elam	Elamites	
Asshur	Assyrians	
Lud	Lydians	
Arphaxad	Chaldeans	
Aram	Arameans	Aramaic
Sin	China	

147

The Unity of Mankind in the Earth is Key to man's Dominion in the Earth

The writer believes that all these nations from the three sons of Noah represent the foundation of unity in the earth. As we've already state above and will now prove, the nations were formed to operate in a divine earthly trinity upon which the earth was to be established, and upon which mankind would have the Psalm 133 commanded blessing released for dominion in the earth.

> *Psa. 133:1 Behold, how good and how pleasant it is for brethren to dwell together in unity! 2 It is like the precious ointment upon the head, that ran down upon the beard, even Aaron's beard: that went down to the skirts of his garments; 3 As the dew of Hermon, and as the dew that descended upon the mountains of Zion: for there the LORD commanded the blessing, even life for evermore.*

Why was the whole earth overspread to three sons? Why didn't Noah have four sons to which the whole earth would be overspread to? , Because mankind was created to relate with one another in the earth as a trinity of nations from Shem, Ham and Japheth. As they would, the earth would receive the commanded blessing of brothers dwelling together in Unity. Why did the 12 tribes of Israel come from the Foundation of Abraham, Isaac and Jacob, why not a fourth patriarch?

The number "3" represents the number of the manifestation of God's oneness and wholeness. *Deut 6:4 Hear O Israel, the Lord our God is One Lord.* The word "ONE" in this verse is the word "Echad" which means to be united. It is the plural word for "One" as in "US" or "We." God has chosen to reveal the mystery of the Godhead as one God through the triune nature of the three persons of the Godhead, Father, Son, and Holy Ghost. One God exists forever as three distinct persons, equal in nature as God and enjoying a deep relationship of love with each other, fully possessing the divine nature, yet differing in function and authority in their relationship and work together, while dwelling in each other. This is also how God created mankind to relate and rule with one another in the earth, as a trinity of nations from Shem, Ham, and Japheth. The significance of the number 3 to God is that it represents immutability. It's an oneness and unity that cannot be broken. (Ecc. 4:12) The number 3 is the number of God's witness and power. It is one of the key essentials of his nature that makes God all powerful. He is all powerful because he is perfectly one within himself, with himself.

The Triune Nature of Man

Man was created in God's image and likeness as a triune being. *Gen 2:7 And the LORD God formed man of the dust of the ground, and breathed into his nostrils the breath of life; and man became a living soul.*

Man was created from the dust of the earth (Body). God breathed into him the breath of Life (Spirit), and man became a living Soul (A life giving personality with individual expression and identity). Our life and life giving nature was dependent upon man maintaining connection with each of these essential properties - *the earth* from which he was formed, and *the God* from which he received his spirit. Both the earth and God together is what formed man's soul - *where he would receive his ability to become a giver of life in the earth, to be fruitful and multiply and replenish the earth.*

A Living Soul

According to Genesis 2:8, to be a living soul (a life giving being), we must stay connected with the earth, or the geographical region from which we received our bodies (physical features). We must also stay in touch with the God from which we received our Spirits (our spiritual features), which is where we receive our ability to be relational and in communion, and unity with God and man. From these two sources, God and the earth coming together within our makeup, we would have the ability to relate with two worlds, the earthly and heavenly realms, enabling us to be fruitful, to multiply and replenish the earth, thusly having dominion in the earth.

The Triune Nature of the Nations: God's governing body in the Earth

At the formation of the nations God was after establishing a governing body in the earth for the accomplishing of his purposes in the earth (man) as it is in heaven (God). Heaven is governed by God which is in perfect unity within his nature, Father, Son and Holy Ghost. Man was created to be governed by his triune nature, Spirit, Soul and Body, with the spirit that comes from God leading the way. And in the formation of the nations it was God's intention for the earth to be governed by an earthly trinity of nations from Noah's three sons, Ham, Shem and Japheth, to which the whole earth would be overspread.

> *Gen 9:19 These are the three sons of Noah: and of them was the whole earth overspread.*

The three sons of Noah represent the tri-unity of mankind's governmental rule in the earth.

In Earth As It Is In Heaven

1Jn 4:17 Herein is our love made perfect, that we may have boldness in the day of judgment: because as he is, (in heaven) so are we in this world.

I John 5:7, 8 say it like this, 7. *For there are three that bear record in heaven, the Father, the Word, and the Holy Ghost: and these three are one.*

8. *And there are three that bear witness in earth, the Spirit, and the water, and the blood: and these three agree in one.*

These three verses show the correlation of heaven and earth and how what's in heaven is connected to and mirrors what's in the earth. When Jesus taught us to pray, he begins by teaching us the connection, mirror principle when he says, Pray, Our father, which art in heaven, Hallowed by thy name, thy kingdom come, *thy will be done, in earth, as it is in heaven*. Heaven and earth were created to mirror one another, and are to be connected to one another. *In the beginning God created the heavens and the earth.* This principle is at the root of the fall and restoration of man and the earth. When man fell he was disconnected from God, his image, and the earth from heaven its' image.

The Mirror Principle of Heaven & Earth

Our prayers are to be focused on bringing these two, man back to God, and heaven back to earth to be united together once again. These two verses in 1 John 5:7, 8 are connected by the conjunction *"and"* to show the mirror principle of how God in heaven functions, and how man in earth is to come to function. Verse 7 says, *there are three that bear record in heaven, the Father, the word, and the Holy Ghost and these three ARE one.*

Verse 8 says, *AND there are three that bear witness in the earth, the Spirit, and the water, and the blood: and these three AGREE in one.*

These three ARE ONE in Heaven

One verse, verse 7, speaking of the Mystery of the Godhead says, *"These three ARE ONE"*, the next verse speaking of man in the earth says, AND...."*these three AGREE IN ONE."* The word "ARE ONE" in verse 7 is the Greek word *"EISI"(pronounced I see)* which means to *"exist," "they are", or "to always have been."* So verse 7 is actually saying, *THESE THREE IN HEAVEN, THE FATHER, THE WORD AND THE HOLY SPIRIT ARE ONE, AND HAVE ALWAYS EXISTED AS ONE.*

These three ARE BECOMING ONE in Earth

In verse 8 the word AGREE IN ONE is stated together unlike verse 7, which simply says, they ARE ONE. But when you put the word "AGREE" with the word "IN," it's the Greek word *"eis"* (pronounced ice) which means *"to", or "into"*. This is indicating a point reached or entered, of time, place or purpose. This makes verse 8 actually say, *"THERE ARE THREE THAT BARE RECORD IN EARTH....AND THESE THREE ARE BECOMING ONE, OR THEY ARE LEARNING TO EXIST AS ONE AS THEY ENTER INTO AND STAY CONNECTED WITH THE THREE IN HEAVEN."* WOW!

Something Happening on Earth that has always been in Heaven

Verse 7 being connected with verse 8 by the conjunction "AND" makes the responsibility of the three in earth to stay connected to the three in heaven in order to learn how to achieve oneness in the earth. It is the purpose of the three in the earth to gaze on, study, investigate, and gain revelation on how the Father, the

Word, and the Holy Ghost operate as one so as to operate as one in the earth. This is achieved by corporate worship. Until the three in earth come together within the body of Christ in worship to agree in one place on who God is and that he's worthy as God to be worshipped, we will never agree in one, and we will never truly understand our purpose. Our purpose is insignificant and impossible without each other. Matthew 18:18-20 says this concerning the body of Christ coming together in one;

> *Mat 18:18 Verily I say unto you, Whatsoever ye shall bind on earth shall be bound in heaven: and whatsoever ye shall loose on earth shall be loosed in heaven. 19 Again I say unto you, That if two of you shall agree on earth as touching anything that they shall ask, it shall be done for them of my Father which is in heaven. 20 For where two or three are gathered together in my name, there am I in the midst of them.*

Here we see the mirror principle of heaven and earth in Matt 18:18 speaking of how the church is to deal with offense and sin that brings division between brothers and sisters in Christ's body. He says, the answer for brothers that are offended with one another and have an aught against another within the body of Christ in the earth is the mirror principle of earth beholding heaven to come into agreement. When we do, he says, I will be in the midst of you. *Where two or three are gathered together in my there am I in the midst of them.* When we don't, he says, that brother that is unwilling to hear the church and agree with God in heaven to resolve the matter causing the offense, treat him as a publican, or a heathen. Why? Because he's hindering the unity and oneness of the body in earth and I can't dwell in your midst unless you come together and agree in earth as it is in heaven. This is the mystery of the Godhead that we are to gaze on, study and learn in order to know how to become one in earth

This mystery has been revealed and will continually be revealed to a people that behold him for the purpose of becoming like him the earth. The purpose of understanding the triune nature of God is to understand how man in the earth is to be in agreement with God and one another to accomplish God's purposes in the earth. As we worship together, all races, nations, ethnicities in one place, in one body we will become one, as God is in heaven, Father Son, and Holy Ghost, one God – and we will come to understand who we are and our purpose in him.

The Mystery of the Godhead reveals our Purpose

The doctrine of the Mystery of the Godhead is one of the most important doctrines in the Bible. In some circles in the body of Christ this mystery is called The Trinity. In other circles this mystery is called The Oneness of the Godhead. Though the word *Trinity* is not in the Bible, its truth is confirmed. *Trinity* means "tri-unity" or "three-in-one." Though the doctrine of the Oneness of God is a valid and true teaching in scripture and interpretation of One God that denies the triune nature of the Godhead is strayed from the Apostolic teachings on the mystery of the Godhead. Over seventy passages in the New Testament present the Father, Son, and Spirit together. This doctrine teaches that God exists as **three persons**—Father, Son, and Spirit. Each distinct person is fully and eternally God, yet there is **only one God.** The mystery of the Godhead is that three divine persons dwell together forever in deep relationship as one God. One God exists forever as three distinct persons, equal in nature as God and enjoying a deep relationship of love with each other, fully possessing the divine nature, yet differing in function and authority in their relationship and work together, while dwelling in each other. What is said about the Godhead and the triune nature of the one God and how the Godhead exists and enjoys a deep relationship of love with each other is what will be said of Man in the earth as we worship him corporately. In understanding the triune nature of the

154

Godhead we can see man's destiny in the earth. There are 7 particular truths about the triune nature of the Godhead that will help as we come together with one another in the earth to become one to accomplish our purpose in the earth. These 7 particular truths are:

1. There is only one God.

2. God forever dwells in three distinct persons who are coequal as divine persons.

3. Each person enjoys an eternal, voluntary, mutual relationship of love, humility and unity.

4. Each person fully possesses all of God's attributes—infinite measure and eternal duration.

5. Each person is different in function and authority in their relationship and work.

6. Each person's work is unified, inseparable, and interdependent with the other's work.

7. Each person mutually dwells in the other two persons.

Using the mirror principle of heaven and earth from I John 5:7,8, Matt 6:10, Matt 18:18-20, I John 4:17 we can gather from the Godhead how God sees the man and the nations that have come from the three sons of Noah in the earth.

1. There is only one Man.

2. Man forever dwells in three distinct persons from Noah's three sons who are coequal as earthly persons.

3. Each person of this earthly union is to enjoy an eternal, voluntary, mutual relationship of love, humility and unity.

4. Each person fully possess all of the others attributes—in measure and increasing towards eternity where it will be without measure

5. Each person is different in function and authority in their relationship and work.

6. Each person's work is unified, inseparable, and interdependent with the other's work.

7. Each person mutually dwells in the other two persons.

Just as there is equality in the Godhead, but differences in the way they relate to each other and function or work in the world so it is with nations from the three sons of Noah. Just as in the Godhead their work includes creation, redemption, and providence (leadership over the nations), with the Father's role being to direct and send, Jesus' role is to obey, pray, and do the Father's work, and the Spirit's role is to apply the work of salvation to us and to anoint us for service, so it is with nations from Noah's three sons. Just as there are differences and roles are not temporary, but will last forever in the Godhead (1 Cor. 15:28), so they will in the nations.

The Witness in Heaven and in Earth

In heaven it takes three to bear record. This is why God is Father, Son and Holy Ghost. God is his own witness in heaven. This is what makes God not need anyone to exist. He exists within himself. He needs no outside agents to exist and make him who he is. The Old folks, growing up in church, used to say it like this, *He's God all by himself, and don't need nobody else.*

The Witness in Man

In the earth man is made up of three that bears record of who he is in this world;
1st witness, <u>*God – The Spirit*</u>, the breath of life.

2nd witness, <u>*The Earth*</u> – his geographical origin from whence comes <u>his body</u>

3rd witness, <u>*His Soul – His personality,*</u> from whence comes his cultural expression. Without man's spirit he dies. Without a body man is not allowed to relate in this earthly realm. Man needs his body to relate in this realm. And without man's soul his earthly, temporal works fail to connect with eternity to produce eternal rewards. These three bear record that man is who he is, and that he is alive.

Witnesses in the Nations

In the nations, the governing of mankind also needs three to bear record, or to witness, in order to accomplish the charge of man from God for the earth. This is why the nations were made up of a trinity of nations from Noah's sons, Ham, Shem and Japheth. As the union of God is three in one, the union of mankind in the earth was meant to be three in one within the body of Christ. All nations came from one of the three sons of Noah; Ham, Shem or Japheth and we were created to be united as one in Christ Jesus in his house of prayer for all nations, ruling and reigning in the earth through the power of governmental high priestly intercession. Noah was a type of Christ, and his three sons were a type of the body of Christ. These three sons were the righteous seed of Noah that God wanted to raise up after the flood. Just as the body of Christ is the righteous seed from Christ on the cross that God raised up after Calvary. The purpose of the flood was not to destroy the earth, but to judge and purge the earth. Just as the purpose of the cross was not destroy God's son, but to judge and purge sin in man. It was for the purpose of exalting righteousness over sin.

In the beginning of the formation of the nations for the accomplishing of the purpose of God for the earth, Noah, found grace in the eyes of God. He would be spared, along with his family, to be the first-fruits of the righteousness of God in the earth. He would be ordained to begin a new order of governmental rule of men in the earth, the time of Human government. Therefore, after the ark was completed God called Noah and his family of righteousness into the ark in order that he might cleanse the earth. After this cleansing process was complete he would release them forth into the entire world in order to reestablish righteousness throughout the land. They would go forth under the original mandate of God to the first man Adam; be fruitful, multiply, replenish the earth and have dominion over it - *Govern the earth and prepare it for God to inhabit once again*. This process will be repeated at the end of the age when God will call those that are righteous into the ark of safety, (His house of Prayer) while he judges, purges and cleanses the earth from sin once and for all, preparing the earth for his habitation. After this cleansing God will send forth his people to go forth once again to be fruitful, multiply and replenish the earth and have dominion over it.

CHAPTER 10

THE PURPOSE AND POWER OF THE RECONCILATION OF NATIONS IN HIS HOUSE OF PRAYER

But now in Christ Jesus ye who sometimes were far off are made nigh by the blood of Christ. 14 For he is our peace, who hath made both one, and hath broken down the middle wall of partition between us...Ephesians 2:13, 14

A new generation of leaders in the twenty-first century is going to need to catch the dream of another king, the King of heaven and earth. In 1963, a dream was espoused by Dr. Martin Luther King Jr. that involved the vision from another King, King Jesus. Martin Luther King had a dream that God could one day remedy the injustice in race relations in the United States of America, by causing justice to roll down like rivers, and righteousness like a mighty stream in our nation and world. Martin Luther King espoused a profound dream of reconciliation of the races that he received from the King of Kings, Jesus Christ. Though this dream was not fully actualized through the life and work of Dr. Martin Luther King Jr. it was initiated through his life to be carried on by forerunners of generations to come. His work began the process toward reconciliation with the desegregation of society in the U.S, bringing down the walls of legislated segregation and separation of the races. This enabled the races the opportunity to become integrated. The picture of the complete dream of Jesus for reconciliation is articulated in Ephesians 2:13-17

But now in Christ Jesus ye who sometimes were far off are made nigh by the blood of Christ. 14 For he is our peace, who hath made both one, and hath broken down the middle wall of partition between us; 15 Having abolished in his flesh the enmity, even the law of commandments contained in ordinances; for to make in himself of twain one new man, so making peace; 16 And that he might reconcile both unto God in one body by the cross, having slain the enmity thereby: 17 And came and preached peace to you which were afar off, and to them that were nigh.

The next generation of leaders must be forerunners; declaring what God wants to do in the twenty-first century upon the earth in bringing the nations together in one new man. I believe that Dr. Martin Luther King Jr. was a major forerunner out of Africa in the 20th century. He is one of the few modeled examples we have in the twentieth century, of the type of leadership that is needed today in the African-American community. During his life he was a voice of reconciliation raised up in our nation. His impact was felt like a ripple effect throughout not only this nation, but also the nations of the world.

I believe that this dream was motivated by the forerunner spirit for the coming together of all nations in his house of prayer, initiated by the mind and heart of God, and articulated through the lips of a man. Dr. King tapped into the heart of God concerning our interaction as people in the nations of the earth, as he sought to side with God on the issues of race, color and injustice. Therefore God used Dr. King in the civil rights movement to begin breaking down the walls of segregation, oppression, and legislated racial discrimination that was in our society and all over the world. As these walls of legal segregation and discrimination came down, it afforded different races the opportunity to have access to each other. God intended this to bring about interaction and dialogue that would one day lead to real reconciliation. I believe that the day and the time for real reconciliation is now, and that God wants to raise up forerunners from all the nations of the earth, to lead with the same visionary zeal and passion in the 21st century as Dr. King in the 20th century. We are entering into the final era of the coming together of the races, which I call **the era of Reconciliation and Fullness**. This is not a work of man, but of God through His body, the church.

The Scriptures say in 2nd Corinthians 5:18, and all things are of God, who hath reconciled us to himself by Jesus Christ, and he has given to us the ministry of reconciliation. What was done in previous generations through the abolishing of slavery, and the struggle for civil rights removing legislated discrimination was not meant to be the completion of this struggle for the coming together and oneness of all people. However, it was the past generation's part that they played preparing the way for the final generation. Now we must take up the baton and mantle of this generation and bring to fullness through the ministry of reconciliation what God began in generations past. *He* hath given to us the ministry of reconciliation.

Reconciliation's Commitment

In scripture, the word "Reconciliation" is the "Greek" word "Kat-Al-Lag-Ay" which means *"exchange" (figuratively adjustment), that is, restoration to (the divine) favor: - atonement, reconciliation (-ing).* Reconciliation is a change from enmity to friendship. It is mutual, i.e., it is a change wrought in both parties who have been at enmity.

(1.) In scripture in <u>Colossians 1:21</u>, <u>Colossians 1:22</u>, the word reconciliation used there refers to a change wrought in the personal character of the sinner who ceases to be an enemy to God by wicked works, and yields up to him his full confidence and love. In <u>2nd Corinthians 5:20</u> the apostle beseeches the

161

Corinthians to be "reconciled to God", i.e., to lay aside their enmity.

(2.) <u>Romans 5:10</u> refers not to any change in our disposition toward God, but to God himself, as the party reconciled. <u>Romans 5:11</u> teaches the same truth. From God we have received "the reconciliation" (R.V.), i.e., he has conferred on us the token of his friendship. So also <u>2Corinthians 5:18</u>, <u>2Corinthians 5:19</u> speaks of a reconciliation originating with God, and consisting in the removal of his merited wrath. In <u>Ephesians 2:16</u> it is clear that the apostle does not refer to the winning back of the sinner in love and loyalty to God, but to the restoration of God's forfeited favor. This is effected by his justice being satisfied, so that he can, in consistency with his own nature, be favorable toward sinners. Justice demands the punishment of sinners. The death of Christ satisfies this justice, and so reconciles God to us. This reconciliation makes God our friend, and enables him to pardon and save us.

In this same manner men and nations must be reconciled to one another. In order for there to be reconciliation there must be exchange, there must be atonement and there must be attitude adjustments to our approach to one another. All of this will lead to the restoration of divine favor in the earth to all humanity. In this final era of Reconciliation and Fullness I believe God is raising up forerunners that will lead His body into this exchange amongst the races, of unconditional love, which is unmerited favor, forgiveness, and consequently the exchange of resources, abilities, giftings, anointings and the hope of Christ's calling for all races in the earth. Thusly bringing forth the coming of a kingdom of Kings and Priests to reconcile heaven and earth and usher Jesus back to the earth. This will be the responsibility of the forerunners from this era of Reconciliation and Fullness.

Reparations from God or Man

As we approach this era of reconciliation and fullness, leaders from this era are going to need to rightly interpret our past oppression and injustice through the mind of God, so that we respond to our former oppressors with the attitude necessary for reconciliation.   We must say to the oppressed, while what's happened to us should not be swept under the rug and forgotten, it must not be harbored as a barrier to Reconciliation. We must know that all things that have happened to us, is going to be answered for someday. We must also know that those things are meant to work for us not against us. Those things were meant to make us better, not bitter. We must further know that someone is keeping account of the hurts and pains that were afflicted upon us by those that have oppressed us. Jesus, the son of God is taking account of everything that we've passed through, as well as how we respond to what we've passed through. Furthermore, it hurts Jesus as much as it hurts us, and he will eventually avenge us. Either through the blood of Jesus or the blood of those that have stood against us and have not repented, there will be reparations.   We must not continue looking to man for reparations.

The totality of the Justice that is needed to make wrong things right cannot come from man, but only from God. Looking to man may restore some natural things lost during those years of oppression, but it cannot restore dignity, self worth, purpose and inner peace. Looking to God for reparations deals, not only with what happened to us naturally, but what happened to our psyche, what happened to our purpose, our initiative and our internal ingenuity. It deals with true Justice which restores the soul of a man, not just the material possessions of a man. Those that look to God for reparations and wait for his Justice will not only receive what man can give, but what only God can give. We must know that God's Justice is the only Justice that can right the wrong done to a man. Jesus is the Justice of God. If those that have hurt any of God's little ones fail to repent and receive Jesus' blood as the payment for their sins against humanity, it will be better for them that a milestone were wrapped around their neck and that they were drowned in the bottom of the sea.

> *Mat 18:6 But whoso shall offend one of these little ones which believe in me, it were better for him that a millstone were hanged about his neck, and that he were drowned in the depth of the sea.*

If those that commit atrocities and sins against humanity repent and receive the blood of Jesus they will be forgiven, and His blood will be the payment for their sins. However, if they won't repent and turn from their oppressive practices, their own blood will be required as payment for their sins. This is how it is for all offences and sins against God and humanity. This, I believe, is what the end-time Judgments at the end of the age are all about, humanities sins against God and one another that have not been submitted to Jesus' Blood. There's a payday coming someday. What those that have been oppressed must do is what Jesus did on Calvary when he was unjustly crucified on the Cross. They must say, father forgive them, for they know not what they do. They must plead not for man's justice, but for the Justice of God.

> *Luk 18:6 And the Lord said, Hear what the unjust judge saith. 7 And shall not God avenge his own elect, which cry day and night unto him, though he bear long with them? 8. I tell you that he will avenge them speedily. Nevertheless when the Son of man cometh, shall he find faith on the earth?*

We must learn to leave the justice and vengeance to God and learn to abide in the Love of God and forgiveness, no matter what has happened to us, or what we have to go through in this life.

Forgiveness and Reconciliation

If we are ever going to be reconciled to God or one another we must learn how to forgive. Matthew 10:6 tells us if we don't forgive our brother of his trespasses, our Heavenly father will not forgive us of our trespasses. Forgiveness is a combination of two words; "Fore" which means forward, or to go before or ahead of, and "Give" which means to offer up. From this etymological word breakdown of forgiveness we can see that forgiveness actually means; *to give beforehand or ahead of the response.* Forgiveness means; *to give or offer reconciliation before there is even the knowledge by the other that there has been a transgression.* Forgiveness is; *to give or offer peace before there is the acknowledgment of an offence.* This is what Jesus did for mankind. He gave to man reconciliation before man had knowledge that there had been a separation. Before we ever came to a realization that we had sinned and had become separated from God as a result of that sin God forgave us. Jesus was the lamb slain before the foundation of the world. He gave us reconciliation beforehand.

How do we Forgive

The nature of God is wrapped up in the meaning of forgiveness. It means to suffer wrong to make right. The word forgiveness means to remit. It means freedom, liberty, to send, to send forth. This is what Jesus did for all humanity on Calvary. He gave beforehand, to send our sins from us. Forgiveness is what released the efficacy of the power of the cross. The first words Jesus spoke on the Cross were the words, *"Father, forgive them; for they know not what they do."* If Jesus would have had un-forgiveness on Calvary his death would have been in vain because his blood would have been incapable of cleansing our sins. His blood would have been sinful. Un-forgiveness is always a product of the sin nature and always leads to bitterness, and offence, which leads to sin. This is what I believe is at the root of some of the problems in certain parts of African-American society. Much of our lawlessness, lasciviousness, and licentiousness is an outgrowth of the sin of un-forgiveness. If we will not forgive those that have misused, mistreated and offended us over the centuries with slavery, discrimination and segregation our un-forgiveness will lead to sin and lawlessness.

In this definition of forgiveness – to give beforehand - we learn how to forgive. We are to forgive before the individual we are forgiving even recognizes they have hurt or offended us. We are to forgive before they even ask for forgiveness. We must forgive not looking for an apology or reparations from those who offended us. This is what Jesus did for us on Calvary. Before we even knew we were sinners he forgave us of our sins, not looking to be repaid for what was done to him. This is how we are to forgive. We are to forgive before anyone ever apologizes for an offence, not to warrant an apology but because we don't need apology.

An Apology's not Necessary

When we actually know what God was doing in us and for us, as well as what God wanted to take us to, through all of the oppression, slavery and discrimination, we will no longer need or want anyone to apologize to us for their actions, or their ancestors actions. One day when we understand what our plight was all about and why we went through what we went through, we will have the response of Joseph when his brothers wanted to apologize to him for selling him into slavery in Egypt in the book of Genesis 50:15-20. The account goes like this

> *15. And when Joseph's brethren saw that their father was dead, they said Joseph will peradventure hate us,*

166

and will certainly requite us all the evil which we did unto him. 16. And they sent a messenger unto Joseph, saying, Thy Father did command before he died, saying,

17. So shall ye say unto Joseph, FORGIVE, I PRAY THEE NOW, THE TRESPASS OF THY BRETHREN, AND THEIR SIN; FOR THEY DID UNTO THEE EVIL: and now, we pray thee, forgive the trespass of the servants of the God of thy father. And Joseph wept when they spoke unto him. 18. And his brethren also went and fell down before his face; and they said, Behold, we be thy servants.

19. AND JOSEPH SAID UNTO THEM, FEAR NOT: FOR AM I IN THE PLACE OF GOD? (Am I not where God wanted me?) 20. BUT AS FOR YOU, YOU THOUGHT EVIL AGAINST ME; BUT GOD MEANT IT UNTO GOOD, TO BRING TO PASS, AS IT IS THIS DAY, TO SAVE MUCH PEOPLE ALIVE.

21. Now therefore fear ye not: I will nourish you, and your little ones. And he comforted them, and spoke kindly unto them.

Joseph's brothers felt that Joseph would treat them wrongly after their father died for what they had done in selling him into slavery. So Joseph's brothers sent messengers to Joseph, saying our father commanded before he died, saying *FORGIVE THE TRESPASS OF THY BRETHREN AND THEIR SIN;* I believe this represents to the African Diaspora world-wide as well as to all those that have ever been offended by their brethren from other races, how God expects us to respond to interracial offence. Our father, which art in Heaven said, to pray like this before he died; *Forgive us our trespasses as we forgive those that trespass against us.* This is what Jesus taught his disciples to pray before he died. Joseph's response is how the African Diaspora will one day respond, both to our African brothers who sold us into slavery and to our former oppressors who enslaved us. When we see what God was doing in us and for us, through our being sold into slavery by our brothers we will respond different to the experience. He said to his brothers, *AM I NOT IN THE PLACE GOD WANTED ME?* God was trying to get some of us out of Africa, into the nations of the world to bring reconciliation, deliverance and fullness. We will one day be able to say as Joseph; *YOU THOUGHT EVIL AGAINST ME; BUT GOD MEANT IT UNTO GOOD, TO BRING TO PASS, AS IT IS THIS DAY TO SAVE MUCH PEOPLE ALIVE.*

When we understand that our slavery was a positioning for us to be deliverers both to our brothers (our race) and to other nations (races), we will no longer need or want to accept apologies for what we've been through. This is what the remainder of this chapter will eventually reveal; what God was doing through our slavery and oppression to position us in the nations of the world for reconciliation and the saving of the nations. Just like Joseph, Jesus doesn't want, nor will he accept our apologies for our sins nailing him to the cross. Jesus wants our reconciliation to God and to one another. The cross was how the enemy of this life, Satan would be defeated, and our sins would be eradicated, setting us free from sins payday of destruction and death. This is what Jesus did for us on Calvary. So ought we to do likewise to our fellowman. Once we forgive God can release our purpose in the earth as well as the power from what we've been through, to accomplish that purpose.

His High calling for us - Jesus

What is the purpose of the nations? When we get to God's purpose for our life everything else will fall in line and begin to work for us. When we talk about God's purpose for the races, we're not speaking of doing for him, but being with Him to become like Him. Being like Jesus in the earth is his high calling on all of our lives. It's what he was hoping for when he called us. What he was hoping for when he saved us was Christ in us the hope of glory. And everything we go through both individually, and as a people is meant to bring us to Christ-likeness. So when Christ saved us he saw us being just like Jesus. He saw us thinking like him, talking like him, walking like him, and living like him. He saved us and prayed over us that God would give unto us the spirit of wisdom and revelation in the knowledge of him: the eyes of our understanding being enlightened; that we might know the hope of his calling. Before we get the good things that we've been promised we've got to become the person that he's been praying for us to become – Jesus, the deliverer.

Returning to our Source

How do you become the person he's been praying for you to become? You must return to the source both in Heaven – Christ, and in the Earth – Your earthly Heritage. We must know what God has called us to do as related to our heavenly, eternal purpose, which deals with our calling to be a priest after the order of Melchizedek, calling heaven to earth, and we must know what God has called us to be after our earthly purpose, which deals with where we've come from in the earth as related to our geographical origin, which releases our earthly heritage. We must study the Son of God, Jesus Christ, to know and enter into our eternal purpose for bringing heaven to earth, and we must study and know where we've come from in the earth as related to the three sons of Noah – Shem, Ham and Japheth, to know where in the body of Christ in the earth we will operate in that purpose.

How do we receive a Revelation of Our Earthly Responsibilities in the Nations (Races)

How do we receive a revelation of our earthly responsibilities in the triune nature of mankind correlated to the triune nature of God? I john 5:8 says, There are three that bear witness in earth, The Spirit, and the Blood, and the Water, and these three agree in one. The Spirit of man in earth comes from the Father, so it correlates to the Father in heaven; the Blood comes from the body of Christ, which was applied to the mercy seat in heaven, so the blood correlates to the Son in heaven. And the Water in the earth comes from the Holy Ghost. John 7:38, 39 says, *He that believeth on me, as the scripture hath said, out of his belly shall flow rivers of living water. 39 (But this spake he of the Spirit, which they that believe on him should receive: for the Holy Ghost was not yet given; because that Jesus was not yet glorified.)* so the Water in the earth correlates with the Holy Ghost in heaven.

Each of these witnesses in the earth, the <u>Spirit</u> – *Father*, the <u>Blood</u> – *the Son*, and the <u>Water</u> – *The Holy Ghost* correlate to one of the three sons of Noah, from which all nations have come from. So if we find out which witness in the earth correlates with which son – Ham, Shem or Japheth, we can find the purpose of the nations by attributing to each son of Noah the purpose in earth of one of the 3 persons in the Godhead in heaven.

Which person of the Godhead relates to the person and purpose of the three sons of Noah? It is my humble opinion that we can find which son of the three sons of Noah correlate to one of the persons of the Godhead by recognizing the sons of Noah that went forth first, second, or third from the land of God-Jerusalem, to rule and attempt to exercise dominion in the earth in the six thousand years of humanity in the earth. Who dwelled and ruled in the land of God the first two thousand years, and which one dwelled and ruled in the land the second two thousand years, and

170

which son went forth in the third two thousand years? We can distinguish the order and purpose of the nations with a Fatherhood anointing, a Son-ship anointing, and a Holy Ghost anointing by determining the order by which they inhabited the land of God. By recognizing the order of the two-thousand year reign of each son of Noah and correlating them to the personalities of each person in the Godhead we can know the general purpose of the nations in the earth.

The Order of the Sons Possessing the Land of God

The nations from Ham were the first inhabitants of what is known now as Jerusalem, the city of God. The land of Israel was originally known as the land of Canaan. Canaan was the fourth son of Ham.

> Genesis 10:15 says, *And Canaan beget Sidon his first born, and Heth* (Hittite tribe from whence cometh Uriah, the husband of Bathsheba) *and the Jebusite, and the Amorite, and the Girgasite, and the Hivite, and the Arkite, and the Sivate. And the Arvadite, and the Zemarite, and the Hanathite and afterward were the families of the Canaanites spread abroad. And the border of the Canaanites was from Sidon, as thou comest to Gerar, unto Gaza; as thou goest, unto Sodom, and Gomorrah, and Admah, and Zeboim, even unto Lasha.* Verse 20, *These are the sons of Ham, after their families, after their tongues, in their countries, and in their nations.*

This land given in Genesis 10:19 is the land now known to us as Jerusalem. It was called during the time of the possessing of the land by the children of Israel the Promise land. It was a land flowing with milk and honey. It was a land of prosperity and blessing, I believe, because of Abraham's encounter in that land with Melchizedek, the priest of the most High God. The land was originally the land of the Canaanites from Ham. After Canaan inhabited the land for approximately two thousand years, it was given by God to Abraham's descendents from Shem. The Children of Israel lived in the land for the next two thousand years, as David established Zion in Jerusalem, until 70A.D. When Jerusalem was destroyed and overrun by the Romans the Japhetic reign began. From this time this land was in the hands of the Europeans from Japheth until God returned the Jews back to their promised homeland Israel, in 1948 and back to Jerusalem as it capital in 1967, after the six day war.

The nations from the three sons of Noah, Ham, Shem and Japheth, are able to see their purpose in the earth as they study the three personalities of the God-head and recognize that not only was man created in His image and likeness, but mankind – *the nations* - were created in His image and likeness. The Father that sent his Son, initiates, imparts and releases *the sowing of the seed* of the word of God, and covers and protects that seed. The Son as God, is the seed sown into the earth. He humbles himself and gives his life for *the reconciling of the World* back to the father. The Holy Ghost as God releases his power to his church, his bride, to be the womb to reproduce the seed sown by the father. He gives this Holy Ghost empowered Church the keys of authority back from Satan, *to subdue the earth*. Each of the nations from the three sons of Noah can find their purpose in the earth as the *Father* that sows the seed, the *Son* that gives his life for the reconciling of the world, or the *Holy Ghost* that unlocks authority to the church to reproduce the seed, to subdue the earth.

The Hametic Purpose – The Fatherhood Covering Anointing – A People of Refuge

In relation to mankind – *the nations* in the earth, being created in the image of God – *Father, Son & Holy Ghost*, and the three sons of Noah, the nations from Ham, having been the first inhabitants of the promise land are in the image of Father. They are initiators in the spirit, Apostolic Fathers, a people of refuge, to cover and preserve, with a fatherhood anointing. As fathers in the nations they have a covering anointing. The fatherhood nations from Ham when restored in the body of Christ with the other two sons, can find their purpose and fulfill their part in the earth coming to its purpose. Matthew 18:20 says where two or three are gathered together in my name there am I in the midst of them. As the sons of Ham are gathered together in the body of Christ with the other two sons from Noah their purpose as Apostolic Fathers in the earth will begin to be seen and manifest in the nations.

The Unique Calling on Africa – Cities of Refuge for Persecuted Jews

Africans around the world have a unique calling at the end of the age. Those from the land of Ham will operate in this fatherhood, covering anointing at the end of the age, ministering to and sheltering Jews in the hour of trial. The Prophet Isaiah in Isaiah 18 clearly gives this message to Africa. It is referring to an area of Africa south of Egypt that is in the general area of Nubia, Sudan, or Ethiopia, and Isaiah 18:7 specifically tells us that these Africans will bring a unique present to the Lord. Zephaniah 3:10 tells us that dispersed Jews will come up from "beyond the rivers of Ethiopia" at the end of the tribulation and this gives us insight into the gift of Isaiah 18:7. The gift that the African people bring the Lord is very likely the gift of Jews sheltered during the final tribulation at the end of the age. Egypt has always been the place of refuge for the Jewish people. It was the place where the nation was built in the centuries before the Exodus. It was also the land that sheltered Jesus when Herod sought to slaughter Him.

> *"When Israel was a child, I loved him, and out of Egypt I called My son". (Hosea 11:1 NKJV)*

The nation of Israel grew as a child in Egypt (Africa) and was then called out during the Exodus under Moses. In the same manner, Jesus was sheltered in Egypt (Africa) as a small child until He was called out of Egypt (Africa) . While these are both fulfillments of Hosea 11:1, there will be a greater fulfillment of Hosea 11:1 at the end of the age. Israel at the end of the age will be a "child" compared to the maturity she will grow to in the Millennium and Jesus will lead the greater Exodus out of Egypt (Africa). The Biblical language around the second coming of Jesus is the language of the Exodus and it will be a second, and greater, exodus led by the greater Moses. Once again Israel, whom God desperately loves, will emerge through Egypt and God will call His Son out of Egypt as Jesus marches out of Egypt as a greater Moses liberating oppressed Jews in prison camps and approaching Jerusalem for the final battle with Jerusalem (Psalm 14:7; 102:13,19, 20; Isaiah 11:11-16; 27:12-13; 42:6-24; 49:5-25; 61:1-2; Jeremiah 30:3-24; 31:1-23; Ezekiel 20:33-44; 39:25-29; Hosea 11:10-11; Micah 4:6; 5:6; 7:12; Amos 9:8-15; Joel 2:32-3:1-2; Zephaniah 3:19-20; Zechariah 9:10-14; 10:10-11;). This will be the ultimate fulfillment of the passage.

The Exodus is the largest single event in the Scripture, about 150 chapters; more than describe the Exodus, are given to describing the ultimate Exodus that will happen at Jesus return. When Hosea 11:1 is viewed in light of Isaiah 18:7 and Zephaniah 3:10 it is easy to see that while the Jews will be specifically "called out of Egypt," Egypt will be the gateway into the whole continent of Africa for Jews in flight at the end of the age and many Jews will travel further south in Africa seeking refuge from the terrors of the great tribulation. The LORD obviously intends both the African people in general and the continent of Africa in particular to take a primary role in ministering to and covering (sheltering) the Jews at the end of the age.

The Fatherhood Anointing Restored to the People of African Descent and their Communities

As African, African-American/Diaspora men & women begin to operate in their true fatherhood anointing, the curse that has been on this people group, as well as in the earth, is going to be broken. God is raising up young African, African-American/Diaspora men to once again walk in the anointing to father - *Protect, And Provide*, both in the natural and the spirit, raising their families, churches, businesses, and nations in the fear and admonition of the Lord. He's turning their hearts back to their children to begin living for the raising up and releasing of sons in the earth. They will begin to walk in their purpose as Apostolic Fathers and Priests praying the priestly prayer of Jesus for unity in John 17.

175

The Urgency of the Crisis

The Scripture is clear that the Jews will face a trial at the end of the age unlike any other in history. Zechariah's description of Israel's trial is terrifying (Zechariah 12-14). Daniel warns that the events will continue until the Jews are scattered (Daniel 12:7). Jesus warns of a time unlike any in human history that would be impossible to survive unless it was shortened. He calls the Jews to run from the city when they begin to see the events unfold (Matthew 24:15-22). Just as Jesus warned, the Jews will have to flee Israel as the antichrist begins to bear down on the land. The critical question is where will the Jews go? The Jews cannot go north. Turkey has traditionally been the seat of the Islamic empire and will not be friendly to Jews in flight. The Jews cannot go east. East is ancient Babylon and modern Islamic nations that will not be friendly to the Jews. Southeast is the land of Arabia, a peninsula consumed with anti-Semitism. The Jews cannot go west because of the Mediterranean. The Jews will be forced to go south through Egypt into Africa. It was 7 lean years of famine that caused Jacob and His sons to go to Egypt before the first Exodus and the last 7 years will create pressure on the earth that will again cause Jacobs sons to flee south to Egypt. Just as He did by sending Joseph, God will prepare intercessors in Egypt to open the door for the Jews to flee to Africa. This time it will be a praying church that opens the heavens over Egypt to provide a moment of safe passage into Africa for the Jews.

However, just as before, Egypt will both shelter and finally oppress the Jews as well, as the antichrist tightens his grip on the Middle East. Because Africa is the only way of escape Jews in the land will have, the religious climate of Africa is an eschatological issue. We must begin to sound an alarm to the church with regard to the crisis that is brewing both in the continent of Africa and among Africans in Diaspora. As friends of the Bridegroom, we must actively participate in His plan to make provision for His brothers in their chief hour of trial.

In the spirit of a forerunner, we must sound an alarm. The implications of Islam's assault on Africans are beyond what we can presently understand. The lack of eschatological understanding has caused us to not perceive what the enemy is doing in our generation. While we want to always carry the Lord's zeal for revival and for the salvation of all people, we must ask some serious questions about the growth of the gospel in Africa as it is related to the Land and people of the promised land.

The Release of the Land to Shem

In relation to mankind – *the nations* in the earth, being created in the image of God – *Father, Son & Holy Ghost*, and the three sons of Noah, after Ham's descendants occupied and lived in the land of God, this land was taken from the Canaanites and promised and given to the seed of Abraham, because of idol worship by the Canaanites in that land. They were to be completely destroyed. Leviticus 18 tells of the sins of the Canaanites.

> Lev.18:1-3, 24, 25 *And the Lord spake unto Moses, saying, Speak unto the children of Israel, and say unto them, I am the Lord your God. After the doings of the land of Egypt, wherein ye dwelt, shall ye not do: and after the doings of the land of Canaan, whither ye go in to possess shall ye not do:*

177

> *for in all these the nations are defiled which I cast out before you: And the lands is defiled: therefore I do visit the iniquity thereof upon it, and the lands itself vomits out her inhabitants.*

The next son of Noah, Shem, begins to arise in the earth through Abraham. Abram was the son of Terah, the son of Nabor, the son of Serug, the son of Reu, the son of Peleg, the son of Eber, the son of Salah, the son of Arphaxad, the son of Shem. Abraham is called and set apart by God to enter into covenant with him in Genesis 12 as Abram.

> *God said unto Abram, Get thee out of thy country, and from thy kindred, and from thy father's house, unto a land that I will shew thee: And I will make of thee a great nation, and I will bless thee and make thy name great; and thou shalt be a blessing: And I will bless them that bless thee, and curse him that curseth thee: and in thee shall all families of the earth be blessed. Genesis 12:1*

The Semitic Purpose – The Son-ship Reconciling Redeeming Anointing

This begins the rise of the second son of Noah, Shem, to begin to be the mighty one in the earth. It was through Abraham's seed that all the nations of the earth would be blessed and reconciled to God. And from his line the Messiah, the Savior of the world would come. It was during this period that the Kingdom of David was established in the earth. This kingdom ruled during his lifetime and his son Solomon's lifetime as the greatest kingdom in the earth. This was the second two-thousand years of the Semitic reign. The Semitic reign represents the second person of the God head, the Son of God, Jesus Christ, whose blood would be shed to take away the sins of the world. So it would be for the descendants of Shem with the Jews and many others of the descendants of Shem. Their casting away (persecution, affliction and tribulation) over the years as a result of Judgment for sin was symbolic and correlates to God's judgment on His Son for the sins of the world, to reconcile the world back to God.

> *Rom 11:12 Now if the fall of them be the riches of the world, and the diminishing of them the riches of the Gentiles; how much more their fulness? 13 For I speak to you Gentiles, inasmuch as I am the apostle of the Gentiles, I magnify mine office: 14 If by any means I may provoke to emulation them which are my flesh, and might save some of them. 15* **For if the casting away of them be the reconciling** *of the world, what shall the receiving of them be, but life from the dead?*

These nations would be nations whose fall would be for the reconciling of the nations. However, their receiving would be life from the dead of the whole earth. In the end they would indeed fulfill the prophecy spoken unto them by God to Abraham, that, *I will bless thee, and make thy name great; and thou shalt be a blessing; and in thee shall all families of the earth be blessed.* The ultimate purpose of the sons from Shem as redeemer, reconciler people will eventually bring together and bless the nations of the world. However, before the blessing there would be the breaking. Before the resurrection there always comes the crucifixion. This first began in Genesis 22:1-8 when Abraham offered up Isaac, the promised seed, unto God on Mount Moriah; because Abraham would be willing to offer up his only son, God cut covenant to release His only Son into the earth. The nations from Shem represent the Son of man through Abraham's seed. They would be seen throughout the lines of time as redeemer nations, that as a result of their casting away they would be for the reconciling of man to God and eventually to one another.

From the purpose of the Son of God, the nations from the sons of Abraham, would find their purpose in the earth. The Son of God said in John 14:6 *I AM the way*, the truth and the life. So it's been for the sons of Abraham, as they have given all religions their great moral code, through the Ten Commandments. The Son came to give His life for the sins of the world. The Son said I *AM the door*. The Son said I *AM the bread of life*. The purpose of the Son is the salvation of the world. From these characteristics of the Son of God and many more, the nations from the sons of Shem can understand their purpose in the earth; fulfill that purpose, coming into unity with the other brothers, Ham and Japheth in the house of prayer to help bring the earth to its destiny and purpose.

The Japhetic Purpose – The Holy Ghost, Helper anointing for the preaching of the Gospel in the whole world

Japheth was the last son of Noah to reign of the three. The scripture declares, the first shall be last, and the last shall be first. Japheth was the eldest, first born son to Noah, but was the last to rule in the earth and occupy the land of God. The baton was passed onto Japheth, in the book of Acts, as Peter was summoned by the Roman Centurion Cornelius, to speak unto him the words of life in Acts 10, and as Paul, the Apostle of Jesus Christ declared His intention and call to the be a light to the Gentiles. It was here that the European nations of the Japhetic line would begin the preaching and spreading of the gospel in the 3rd two-thousand year period.

Peter unlocks the door to the Gentiles to receive the message and mantle for the spreading of the gospel in Acts 10:1

Acts 10:1 There was a certain man in Caesarea called Cornelius, a centurion of the band called the

> *Italian band, 2 A devout man, and one that feared God with all his house, which gave much alms to the people, and prayed to God always. 3 He saw in a vision evidently about the ninth hour of the day an angel of God coming in to him, and saying unto him, Cornelius. 4 And when he looked on him, he was afraid, and said, what is it, Lord? And he said unto him, Thy prayers and thine alms are come up for a memorial before God. 5 And now send men to Joppa, and call for one Simon, whose surname is Peter: 6 He lodges with one Simon a tanner, whose house is by the sea side: he shall tell thee what thou oughtest to do.*

Paul's Call to the Gentiles in Acts 13:46-48

> *Then Paul and Barnabas waxed bold, and said, It was necessary that the word of God should first have been spoken to you: but seeing ye put it from you, and judge yourselves unworthy of everlasting life, lo, we turn to the Gentiles. 47 For so hath the Lord commanded us, saying, I have set thee to be a light of the Gentiles, that thou shouldest be for salvation unto the ends of the earth. 48 And when the Gentiles heard this, they were glad, and glorified the word of the Lord: and as many as were ordained to eternal life believed.*

With this release and baton handoff made to the Japhetic - *European nations* - that had begun ruling, reigning and attempting to take dominion in the earth, with the rise of Alexander the Great in 300 B.C., the gospel began to be spread throughout the known world, to Jew and Gentile alike. And even though the Roman Empire and many other European dynasties went forth to conquer and overrun the nations from Ham and Shem in the 3rd

two-thousand years, they also carried the mantle and message of the gospel in this 3rd two-thousand year period, keeping the light of the message of salvation through Jesus Christ shining to be given to the ends of the earth. Each son from Noah has taking turns attempting to overthrow, overtake and oppress the other two sons, to have dominion in the earth. However, each son has also taking turns in helping take the message of a coming savior to the world.

It was the European nations from Japheth that would take the gospel throughout world in the last 2000 years and be responsible for spreading it to the four corners of the earth. It would be the European Nations from Japheth that would reign in the earth over this last 2000 year period. It would be these nations that would take the gospel back to the dark regions of Africa and renew and restore the Christian faith that was lost during the 7th century onward when Muslims begin to violently spread Muhammad's religion of Islam throughout Africa. As the result of the loss of an expression of the Christian faith in the regions of Africa, the regions on this continent would be darkened for centuries with witch-craft and necromancer and indigenous religions. These European Nations from Japheth would represent the power and anointing of the third person of the Godhead, the Holy Ghost to be released as rivers of living water throughout the world. They would be most responsible for the spread of the gospel to the four corners of the earth. The European nations from Japheth would be missionary nations that would send missionaries all over the globe with the message of Jesus Christ's death burial and resurrection. They would be the distributors of the Gifts to the Nations in the last 2000 years. They would be the Helper nations that would be the possessors of the wealth for the taking of the gospel to the ends of the earth in the last 2000 years. They would be the nations that would make intercession by the spirit for the other two sons to come to the knowledge of Jesus Christ through missionaries being sent throughout the world.

182

> *Rom 8:26 Likewise the Spirit also helpeth our infirmities: for we know not what we should pray for as we ought: but the Spirit itself maketh intercession for us with groanings which cannot be uttered.*

The nations from Japheth would have the mantle in the last 2000 years to unlock the door of the Gospel to the earth. Just as the nations from the Hametic peoples were the predominant son in the earth in the first two thousand years, and just as the nations from the Semites were the predominant son in the second 2000 years, the Europeans from Japheth would be the predominant son instrumental in the preaching of the gospel in the entire world in the third 2000 years. Even though the gospel, in many cases was spread through the oppression of slavery and colonialism, it was none the less spread. God had a plan in the slavery of the African nations by the Europeans, just as God had a plan in the slavery of the Jews in Egypt, an African nation – *The Worship of Jehovah God.* God did not enslave any people, but he did allow it to accomplish his purposes. He allowed it to cause the children of Israel in Egypt to cry out to him for deliverance. And he allowed it to get those from the nations from Ham to cry out to Him, and to get those of the nations from Ham all over the world, into all the nations of the world. He allowed it so that Africans, who were in Islam or dark, indigenous, ancestral worship of devils, or nature, or animals, would hear the gospel preached to them by their Japhetic, European brothers and cry out to Jesus, the true and the living God, for the deliverance. This preaching of the gospel in Africa and in the European nations of the world would be strategic at the end of the age for that continent to be able to fulfill their Apostolic covering anointing as cities and places of Refuge for Jews in flight at the persecution of the Anti-Christ during the last 3 ½ years of human history.

My House shall be Called the House of Prayer

CHAPTER 11

PRAYING CHURCH PRINCIPLE # 6 - Power in The House
– The Mountain of the Lord's house

Mat 21:14 And the blind and the lame came to him in the temple; and he healed them.

Power like has not been seen in the church in its 2000 year history is coming to the end-time House of Prayer as God's house embraces it's call to Jesus, and His mission to and for *all nations*. Power in the house of God can only be seen where there is the Unity of the races of People in the house of God that gives man an Encounter with the Glorified Christ. When Jesus went into the temple and cleansed out the money changers and religious systems, **they brought to him** *the lame and the blind and HE HEALED THEM there*. Power is always the natural result of bringing the world to an encounter with the Glorified Christ. This end-time church is going to present to the world an encounter with the Glorified Christ bringing them to God, not a man, to be healed of her sickness, immorality, racism and pride. As a result of being brought to an encounter with the Glorified Christ, she will walk in a level of power beyond anything seen in church history, that no disease known to man will be able to stand in the presence of the people of God.

At the International House of Prayer God gave the community the word that in this end-time prayer movement when God begins to raise up the worshippers, singers, and intercessors together in a community of prayer, faith and worship God will release his healing power in such a way that no disease known to man will be able to stand in the presence of this people. What is the secret to power on this level? How did Jesus walk in a power where he healed them all? We must encounter the Glorified Christ.

The Secret to the Power of Prayer

Mark 9:1-8; 27-29 *This kind can come out only by Prayer*

The Power of Prayer is directly related to an Encounter in Prayer. Jesus relates this truth in Mark 9:14 when Jesus came to a boy who was possessed by a spirit.

> *Mar 9:17 And one of the multitude answered and said, Master, I have brought unto thee my son, which hath a dumb spirit; 18 And wheresoever he taketh him, he teareth him: and he foameth, and gnasheth with his teeth, and pineth away: and I spake to thy disciples that they should cast him out; and they could not. 19He answereth him, and saith, O faithless generation, how long shall I be with you? how long shall I suffer you? bring him unto me.*

> *20 And they brought him unto him: and when he saw him, straightway the spirit tare him; and he fell on the ground, and wallowed foaming. 21 And he asked his father, How long is it ago since this came unto him? And he said, Of a child. 22 And ofttimes it hath cast him into the fire, and into the waters, to destroy him: but if thou canst do any thing, have compassion on us, and help us. 23 Jesus said unto him, If thou canst believe, all things are possible to him that believeth.*

> *Mar 9:24 And straightway the father of the child cried out, and said with tears, Lord, I believe; help thou mine unbelief. 25 When Jesus saw that the people came running together, he rebuked the foul spirit, saying unto him, Thou dumb and deaf spirit, I*

186

charge thee, come out of him, and enter no more into him. 26 And the spirit cried, and rent him sore, and came out of him: and he was as one dead; insomuch that many said, He is dead. 27 But Jesus took him by the hand, and lifted him up; and he arose. 28 And when he was come into the house, his disciples asked him privately, Why could not we cast him out?

Mar 9:29 <u>And he said unto them, This kind can come forth by nothing, but by prayer.</u>

Now we must qualify what type of prayer Jesus was referring to when he says "this kind can come forth by nothing but by prayer." When Jesus makes this statement on the surface it would seem to infer that any ole prayer would suffice to produce the power needed for the dumb and deaf to be delivered and healed. But Jesus wasn't referring to our religious prayer meetings, nor was he referring to our prayer recitals that we imagine when we think of reciting the Lord's Prayer in Matthew 6, and Luke 11. However, He gives us a glimpse into the type of prayer he was referring to in the context of this text beginning in Mark 9:2 and in Luke's account of this story in Luke 9:28.

Encountering the Glorified Christ in Prayer

Mar 9:2 And after six days Jesus taketh with him Peter, and James, and John, and leadeth them up into an high mountain apart by themselves: and he was transfigured before them. 3 And his raiment became shining, exceeding white as snow; so as no fuller on earth can white them. 4. And there appeared unto them Elias with Moses: and they were talking with Jesus.

Luk 9:28 And it came to pass about an eight days after these sayings, he took Peter and John and James, and went up into a mountain to pray. 29 And as he prayed, the fashion of his countenance was altered, and his raiment was white and glistering. 30 And, behold, there talked with him two men, which were Moses and Elias: 31 Who appeared in glory, and spake of his decease which he should accomplish at Jerusalem. But Peter and they that were with him were heavy with sleep: and when they were awake, they saw his glory, and the two men that stood with him.

From these passages in Mark 9 and Luke 9 we can see that when Jesus said that this kind of power can only be released by prayer, he was talking about an Encounter in prayer with a person. He was speaking about prayer that encounters the Glorified Christ and sees the beauty and glory of God in prayer. This type of prayer is missing in the modern church of our generation. Therefore this type of power is missing from the church of this generation. Paul records a glory encounter with the glorified Christ that empowered him to do all that God had called him to do in the earth in Acts 26:13-18.

Act 26:13 At midday, O king, I saw in the way a light from heaven, above the brightness of the sun, shining round about me and them which journeyed with me. 14 And when we were all fallen to the earth, I heard a voice speaking unto me, and saying in the Hebrew tongue, Saul, Saul, why persecutest thou me? it is hard for thee to kick against the pricks. 15 And I said, Who art thou, Lord? And he said, I am Jesus whom thou persecutest. 16 But rise, and stand upon thy feet: for I have appeared unto thee for this purpose, to make thee a minister

> *and a witness both of these things which thou hast seen, and of those things in the which I will appear unto thee; 17 Delivering thee from the people, and from the Gentiles, unto whom now I send thee, 18 To open their eyes, and to turn them from darkness to light, and from the power of Satan unto God, that they may receive forgiveness of sins, and inheritance among them which are sanctified by faith that is in me.*

Paul goes on to say as a result of this encounter:

> *Whereupon, O king Agrippa, I was not disobedient unto the heavenly vision. (Acts 26:19)*

How did Paul have the power to fulfill the Heavenly vision? Paul had a visitation from Heaven. Paul encountered the Glorified Christ. Therefore he had the power to do all that God had commissioned him to do. Our Power to do and be all that God has called us to do and be is found in an encounter with the Glorified Christ.

In Psalm 27:4 David said, one thing Have I desired of the Lord...to behold the beauty of the Lord. Again in our generation, as in David's, the Holy Spirit is orchestrating a worldwide worship movement that is essential in releasing God's beauty and power in the nations. The power of God is not just going to break out, and then, suddenly the great harvest will happen. Before the second coming, God's power is going to break out, in relation to a global prayer and worship movement. It is happening right now; it is all over the world.

Here is the key point: this movement is fueled by the revelation of encountering the beauty of God. David's prayer ministry was fueled by this revelation of encountering the beauty of God.

Towards this end David had 4,000 musicians who were full-time singers that worshipped 24/7 committed to this – Beholding (encountering) the Beauty of the Lord. Lord raise up your singers, worshipers & intercessors in an end-time day & night prayer & worship movement committed to beholding your beauty. If we're going to see the power in prayer that Jesus promised us, we must seek and receive an encounter with God in prayer. God spoke to my heart one day in prayer and said, "**Brondon, when I am your reward in prayer, I will reward your prayers with Power.**"

God told Abraham something similar to this in Genesis 15:1, saying, *I am thy great reward.*

> *"After these things the word of the LORD came unto Abram in a vision, saying, Fear not, Abram: I am thy shield, and thy exceeding great reward."*

God wants to be our reward in prayer, his very presence, his very person, him showing us His glory, as we seek his face, not his hand. Psalm 24:6 David said this glory encounter generation would be characterized by a generation that seeks him, that seeks his face. This was also Moses prayer and heart after God. Moses was actually the first to desire a glory, beauty encounter in Psalm 90 praying in verse 17 "may the beauty of the Lord our God rests upon us; establish the work of our hands for us, yea the work of our hands establish thou it. And in Exodus 33:13-15 Moses prayed;

> *Now therefore, I pray thee, if I have found grace in thy sight, shew me now thy way, that I may know thee, that I may find grace in thy sight: and consider that this nation is thy people. And he said, My presence shall go with thee, and I will give you rest. **And he said unto him, If thy presence go not with me, carry us not up hence.***

When He is our reward in prayer he will reward our prayers with Power. When we encounter his beauty in prayer he will establish the work of our hands.

The Prayer Climb up the Mountain of Encounter

This Power in prayer comes with the invitation of Jesus in Mark 9:3 to encounter the glorified Christ. *After so many days Jesus took Peter, James and John and led them up a high mountain to pray.* If we're going to have an encounter with Jesus there are several things that we must focus on from these passages in Mark and Luke as we follow Jesus up the mountain to encounter:

1. We must let him "**take us,**" all of us. *WE MUST BE TAKEN BY HIM*, spirit, soul and body. This verse said, "*After so many days Jesus **took** Peter, James and John...What does it take to be taken by Jesus?* It is the Greek word – para lam banō - which means -*to receive near, that is, associate with oneself (in any familiar or intimate act or relation); by analogy to assume an office; figuratively to learn: - receive, take (unto, with).* We must associate ourselves with Jesus in an intimate way that we might be completely and totally obedient to him, doing all he tells us to do, totally surrendered. When we get to the place where we are letting Jesus take us we're on our way to an encounter with the glorified Christ.

2. Next after he takes us we must let him *lead us*. When we are taken by Jesus he's able to lead us to a place in prayer that is guided by him. We don't encounter him in prayer because we don't let him lead us in prayer. We don't let him lead our prayers. Romans 8:26 says, *we don't know what we should pray for as we ought; but the spirit himself makes intercession for us with groanings that cannot be uttered.* We want to pray about everything else but what he wants us to pray about. But when he leads us in prayer we will be directed in our prayers to pray what he wants, not what we want. The Greek word for to "lead up" is a

191

word *"an-af-er-o,"* which means to offer up. We must let him offer us up that our prayers will be received and answered in the earth. Our prayer life must be a sacrificial offering up of our lives and bodies to him that we might be vessels unto honor that he can pray his will through for the earth.

3. When we let him lead us in prayer, He will lead us up into the mountain of prayer. **We must enter into the mountain of prayer, which represents the spirit world, to receive the power of prayer.** The text said, *"He led them up into a high mountain to **pray"***. To come into the mountain of prayer is more than a place of saying a prayer recital. Going into a mountain to pray is symbolic of going from one kingdom into another kingdom for an extended time in the presence of God. Mountains in scripture represent kingdoms. When he leads us up into a mountain he's taking us from one world, the natural world in prayer, to the spirit world in prayer. This is not a quick thing that we can do in a minute or an hour, but we need an extended time of prayer. When Jesus went up into a mountain to pray he was usually there all night in prayer. Isaiah 56:7 says, Even them shall I bring to my holy mountain, and I will make them joyful in my house of prayer. The house of prayer paradigm is all about the church becoming joyful in the end-time mission of prayer. When we become joyful in the house of prayer we will become a mighty mountain in the earth. When we become a house of prayer all the nations will flow into his Holy Mountain. Isaiah 2:2-5 says:

> *Isa 2:2 And it shall come to pass in the last days, that the mountain of the LORD'S house shall be established in the top of the mountains, and shall be exalted above the hills; and all nations shall flow unto it. 3 And many people shall go and say, Come ye, and let us go up to the mountain of the LORD, to the house of the God of Jacob; and he will teach us of his ways, and we will walk in his paths: for out*

192

of Zion shall go forth the law, and the word of the LORD from Jerusalem. 4 And he shall judge among the nations, and shall rebuke many people: and they shall beat their swords into plowshares, and their spears into pruninghooks: nation shall not lift up sword against nation, neither shall they learn war any more. 5 O house of Jacob, come ye, and let us walk in the light of the LORD.

We won't encounter God in prayer without letting him have our lives, our bodies and our time, letting him have a set aside time of hours, days, and seasons of prayer. Until we let Jesus take us up into the mountain of prayer for extended seasons of prayer by the spirit we will not encounter him. And No encounter, No power.

Alone on the Mountain with the Glorified Christ

Again in Mark 9:4 it says when they were all alone, there he was transfigured before them. His clothes became dazzling white, whiter than anyone in the world could bleach them. And there appeared before them Elijah, and Moses who were talking with Jesus. I heard a preacher say once, "We must learn to get alone with God until we're not alone anymore." When they got alone with God for an extended season of prayer they were no longer alone anymore. They began to see the Glorified Christ, the eternal Christ that was before the world began, conversing with Elijah and Moses. I believe this represents the power of the spirit that's coming from an end-time encounter with Jesus in prayer in the days to come. I believe in the end time prayer movement God is releasing the power of the spirit of Elijah and Moses back to our churches and prayer meetings.

The Spirit of Moses and Elijah on the End-Time Praying Church

The picture we will get and the impartation we will receive from the end-time praying church will be like that seen on Moses and Eljiah. We will have the spirit of confrontation to deal with sin, sickness, evil and an ungodly church and political system that will be challenged by the end time prayer movement. As they were in the prayer movements seen both in Moses' day in Egypt and in Elijah's day in Israel, the end-time church is going to have power to confront sin and Satan himself. As Elijah on Mt Carmel, challenging the ungodly, wicked, religious system in Israel of the prophets of Baal, and as Moses in Egypt challenging Pharaoh's system of oppression and slavery, the spirit of the Prophets Moses and Elijah will come on the end-time praying church. It will come on the Church for the operation of the prophetic that we will see released and raised up in the church. This Spirit will return His church to a House of Prayer, releasing the judgments on the religious and political systems of these last days. This prophetic spirit of Moses and Elijah that is coming on the end-time prayer movement in His house of prayer is going be the spirit that prepares the church to confront the Anti-Christ system of the last days and stand in the face of persecution and death unflinching and unrelenting, releasing the end-time Judgments on the world recorded in the book of the Revelation and in book of Daniel. The Church does not have this end-time spirit yet because we have not had a power encounter with the glorified Christ in prayer.

Acts 1:8 says, *after the Holy Ghost has come upon us we would receive power, and we would be witnesses unto him beginning in Jerusalem.* Why Jerusalem? What does Jerusalem represent? Jerusalem is not only the City of David, but it's the city of evil, satanic, religious systems that will eventually be stirred up by the witness of Christ and his church to reach a crescendo of evil and opposition to God in the last days. The word witness is the Greek word *"martis"* which is where we get the word martyr. Which is someone willing to die for what he believes in. Jerusalem is the place where martyrs die. Jerusalem is the capital of a political and religious system that will eventually end with the blood of the martyrs of the souls on the altar in heaven praying for vengeance from their bloodshed in Jerusalem for the establishment of Joy, peace and righteousness in the Holy Ghost.

> ***Rev 6:9, 10*** *And when he had opened the fifth seal, I saw under the altar the souls of them that were slain for the word of God, and for the testimony which they held: And they cried with a loud voice, saying, How long, O Lord, holy and true, dost thou not judge and avenge our blood on them that dwell on the earth?*

Jerusalem is the place where Jesus knew he would go to die and shed his blood for the sins of the world. He was prepared for this mission as a martyr in Jerusalem through his mountain encounter experiences when he met with Moses and Elijah in the glory of God.

> *Luk 9:28-31 And it came to pass about an eight days after these sayings, he took Peter and John and James, and went up into a mountain to pray. And as he prayed, the fashion of his countenance was altered, and his raiment was white and glistering. And, behold, there talked with him two men, which were Moses and Elias:* ***Who appeared in glory, and spake of his decease which he should accomplish at Jerusalem.***

Jesus' encounters in the glory prepared him to release power to live and power to die. Right now in the modern western church we're not able to face much persecution or look in the face of death with the prayers and power of a martyr because we are missing the power of encounter in the place of prayer. That's why we've embraced wholeheartedly a pre-trib rapture theology that has us looking to escape persecution and opposition rather than face it head on with the victory which is in Christ Jesus. God did not leave His Church here to legislate the Kingdom on earth, only to have Jesus "snatch" us away because Satan was simply too much for us. Either Satan is under our feet, or not. So, please Church, unpack your bags, and quit being lazy and fearful and take dominion and authority through prayers of encounter .... NOW! As we come down to the last days right before the coming of the Lord we are being positioned to encounter him that we might receive the spirit of Moses and Elijah to confront powers and systems of darkness to prepare the way of the Lord and His coming kingdom to the earth. As we encounter the Glorified Christ we will receive a spirit of boldness and authority to endure the attacks and persecution of the wicked one.

The Hour at Hand

John 16:20 I tell you the truth, you will weep and mourn while the world rejoices. You will grieve, but your grief will turn to joy. A woman giving birth to a child has pain because her hour has come: but when her baby is born she forgets the anguish because of her joy that a child is born into the world.

When Jesus was glorified he was not only being empowered to heal the sick, he was being empowered to endure his hour at hand to suffer, die and be resurrected. What does this hour at hand entail? First of all, if an individual, ministry, or business is going to go up into new levels of spiritual, financial, and material increase in responsibility, stewardship, and ownership, they are

196

going to have to face and go through the circumstances that surround the hour at hand. Many people stay on one or two levels all of their lives because they don't understand the hour at hand and how to respond during this time. Many that desire growth and increase will never increase beyond where they are because they fail to respond correctly to the hour at hand.

Encounter prayer is the only way to endure this time and respond correctly. Why do ministries stay on one level and never breakthrough to new levels? They don't watch and pray for their hour at hand. Why do families stay on one level and never breakthrough to new levels? They don't watch and pray for their hour at hand. The circumstances that surround your *hour at hand* involves weeping, lamenting, sorrow, travail, anguish, suffering of the cross, sacrificial giving of self, and the like. However the end result is joy, rejoicing, delivery, receiving, abundance and the like. What those that are not careful to let God take them into the mountain of prayer miss is that you will never get to the place of the glory realm if you don't go through the hour at hand. *Everything you're going through is for what you're about to go to.* The pain, suffering and anguish of breaking out of the past ways, habits, mindsets and surroundings is necessary if you're going to get from the present level into the promise of the next level. In order to receive from Jesus in prayer when we pray in His name the Bible says we must go through the sorrow, pain and anguish of the birthing process from this present life and level to the next level of life and living promised us.

The Source of Power in the Name of Jesus

The verse in John 16:23, 24 that follows the verse on the sorrow of a woman in travail says:

> *And in that day (what day? The day of delivery out of the time of anguish, pain and travail to the day of joy and rejoicing) ye shall ask me nothing. Verily, verily, I say unto you, Whatsoever ye shall ask the Father in my name, he will give it you. Hitherto have ye asked nothing in my name: ask, and ye shall receive, that your joy may be full.*

Many people wonder why when they pray in Jesus' Name they do not receive what they ask. One reason why might be because they're not in Jesus' Name. In order to pray in Jesus' Name you must be *in* Jesus' Name. You don't get in Jesus' Name by magic words or confession alone. You don't get in Jesus' Name by believing alone. You have to be birthed through travail into the Name of Jesus through the trials, suffering, and tribulations of life. Confession and faith in His Word should impregnate you and bring you to the birth canal; but, travail and intercessory prayer is what's going to get you through the birth canal. It's in the birth canal of travail and intercessory prayer that we get revelation that breaks us through into the next level. It's in the mountain of travail and intercessory prayer that we gain access into the place of grace and abundance.

> Romans 5:1-3 says, *Therefore being justified (qualified, declared legal and innocent) by faith (revelation of Jesus) we have peace (relationship, reconciliation) with God through our Lord Jesus Christ. By whom also we have access (an open door) by faith (revelation) into this grace (abundance of favor) wherein we stand, and rejoice*

198

in hope (confident expectancy of a desired end) of the glory of God (the word made flesh). And not only so, but we glory in tribulations also: knowing that tribulation works (employs) patience (constant endurance in good and bad times); and patience, experience; and experience, hope; and hope makes not ashamed; because the love of God is shed abroad in our hearts by the Holy Ghost which is given unto us.

Travailing Prayer Not an Event, but a Season

When you mix your ability to patiently endure trying times and your experiences that you have previously endured together with the qualities of hope and the love of God, you'll see the power in prayer when you use the Name of Jesus. Through intercessory prayer and travailing into the Name of Jesus, you now have access by faith into the grace of God to see your desires granted and God move on your behalf.

But most people never make it through the season of travail, anguish, and suffering to get to this place, because they fail to watch and pray for the hour at hand that they might respond correctly in these times of trial and tribulation. Many Christians get offended during these times. Many Christians complain, murmur and grumble to God during these times. Many Christians are tempted to curse God and die spiritually during these times. This hour of the season of birthing is not meant to cause you to abort God's purposes for your life. This is not a time to become offended and backslide. This is a time to pray and fast for the next level of God's purposes for your life and ministry. Intercessory prayer and travail is not a one-time event in prayer in which you're moaning and groaning. It could be that kind of an experience in prayer, but most often it is a season of pain, a season of suffering, a wilderness season, a season of tribulation that brings you to a place of fervency and urgency in prayer that causes you to press into the Kingdom of God in a new dimension. It's a season that causes you to seek God with all your heart. It's a season that drives you to God like no other time before. It's a season of tribulation meant to bring you forth into a new dimension in God. Acts 14:22 says, we must through much tribulation enter into the Kingdom of God. The word *tribulation* is the Greek word *thlibo*, which means narrow, pressure, to crowd. This is the same word that is used in Matthew 7:14 when it says, *Because strait is the gate, and narrow is the way, which leads to life, and few there be that find it.* The word *narrow* is also the Greek word *thlibo*, and it is referring to a constricted place, a birth canal. It is this mountain top season of encountering the glorified Christ and this season of suffering, persecution and tribulation that brings you out of one level and dimension into a whole new level of power for life and living.

Responsibilities and Requirements When Your Hour is at Hand

1. Watch & Pray
2. Surrender (To the will of God)
3. Resist temptation in the flesh
4. Forgive those that betray and forsake you (Judas)
5. Give sacrificially (The Cross)

To go to the next level in Christ you must go through the cross. After your greatest time of sacrifice, or sacrificial giving you will experience a resurrection and glorification that will take you into your destined place of glory and power in the presence of God, ministry and promised blessing. It was after the cross that Jesus was restored to His place and position at the right hand of the Father. It was after the offering up of Isaac that Abraham was given his place and position of fruitfulness, and blessing as the father of the faith of many nations.

200

CHAPTER 12

PRAYING CHURCH PRINCIPLE # 7 - Praise in the House - *The Glorified Church*

> *Mat 21:16 And said unto him, Hearest thou what these say? And Jesus saith unto them, Yea; have ye never read, Out of the mouth of babes and sucklings thou hast perfected praise?*

As a result of His body encountering Him in the mountain of prayer, God will raise up his church to be a praise in the earth, and all men will glorify and praise the King of Kings and the Lord of Lords. In the last days the Praying Church will also be known as a Praising Church. True encounter Prayer always leads to awe, to intimate worship and High Praise. And awe, intimate worship and high praise always leads to the execution of the purposes and judgments of God for the earth. When the church encounters the glorified Christ, Christ will glorify His church in the earth to accomplish all of his will. When Christ glorifies His Church in the earth, she will begin to establish His will, and His judgments against his enemies. One of the weapons in the end times that will be utilized by the Praying Church against the enemies of God will be the weapons of Praise & Worship in the house of prayer. Psalm 149:6 Says,

> *Let the high praises of God be in their mouth, and a two edged sword in their hand; 7 To execute vengeance upon the heathen, and punishments upon the people; 8 To bind their kings with chains, and their nobles with fetters of iron; 9 To execute upon them the judgment written: this honour have all his saints. Praise ye the LORD.*

201

At the International House of Prayer we look at the House of Prayer as the governmental center of the universe. From this governmental center will be a "Prayer Ministry" that worships and praises the King of kings in the earth, which includes all the Spirit inspired prayers on earth and in heaven that converge before God. God's government flows from prophetic worship based on the beauty of holiness. God is restoring the spiritual weapons of worship with intercession in prophetic worship. The End of the Age government and power is linked to singers and musicians. The Davidic Church is one that functions as a house of prayer. It is remarkable how central singers are to the End of the Age drama.

Corporate intercessory worship is the *primary means* God has chosen to release His government (power). It is the highest expression of His government in time and eternity and is the most powerful weapon that exists. It is the front line of defense in our war against darkness. The NT Church sowed the seed of God's order of worship as first established on earth in David's Tabernacle using psalms, hymns, and spiritual songs (Eph 5:18-19; Col. 3:16; Jas. 5:13).

> *14 Simon (Peter) declared how God...visited the Gentiles to take out of them a people for His name. 15 With this the words of the prophets agree, as it is written: 16 "After this I will return and will rebuild the Tabernacle of David, which has fallen down; I will rebuild its ruins, and I will set it up; 17 so that the rest of mankind may seek the LORD..." (Acts 15:14-17)*

Church history parallels Israel's history. Whenever God released a season of revival to restore what was lost, we see the aspects of David's order of worship released in that generation. Every revival in history has received an aspect of God's "new song and music" for that generation.

David's Vow will be expressed in the End-Time Worship Movement

When we add one billion believers (currently on earth) to one billion new converts there will be more of God's people on earth than in heaven. In light of this, there may be more prayer for the release of the Kingdom on earth in the final years of natural history than all history combined.

The Holy Spirit's End-Time movement (Rev. 22:17; 5:8; 8:4; Lk. 18:7-8; Mt. 25:1-13; Isa. 62:6-7; 24:14-16; 25:9; 26:8-9; 27:2-5, 13; 30:18-19; 42:10-13; 43:26; 51:11; 52:8; Joel 2:12-17, 32; Jer. 31:7; Mic. 5:3-4; Zeph. 2:1-3; Ps. 102:17-20; 122:6; Zech. 12:10, etc.).

The Millennium is a 1,000-year period in which Jesus will rule the whole world from Jerusalem in righteousness and peace. At this time the Kingdom of God will be openly manifest worldwide affecting every sphere of life (political, social, agricultural, economic, spiritual, educational, law enforcement, media, arts, technology, environment, social institutions, etc.). Isa. 2:1-4; 9:6-9; 11:1-16; 60-62; 65:17-25; Ps. 2; 110; Mt. 5:5; 6:10; 17:11; 19:28; 28:19; Acts 1:6; 3:21).

> *4 I saw thrones, and they (saints) sat on them...They lived and reigned with Christ for 1000 years...6 They shall reign with Him 1000 years. (Rev. 20:4-6)*

The kings of the earth will be saved and worship Jesus (Ps. 72:11; 102:15; 138:4; 148:11; Isa. 62:2; Rev. 21:24) and base their national governments on God's Word.

> *11 All kings shall fall down before Him; all nations shall serve Him. (Ps. 72:11)*

The End-Time worship movement will call Jesus to the earth at the time of the Second Coming. The Millennial worship movement will call the Father to the earth (Rev. 21:3). For the first time, the Spirit will universally emphasize our spiritual identity as Jesus' Bride. The Holy Spirit's worship movement will reach a great crescendo just prior to Jesus' Second Coming as the Spirit and the Bride cry out for Jesus to come to establish His Kingdom.

> *17 The Spirit and the Bride say, "Come!"...20 He (Jesus) who testifies to these things says, "Surely I am coming quickly." Amen. Even so, come, Lord Jesus! (Rev. 22:17, 20)*

1). "Jesus, Come near us (intimacy)"
2). "Jesus, Come to us (revival)"
3). "Jesus, Come for us (Second Coming)"

The End-Time prayer and worship movement will be mature and operate in great authority with a bridal identity (Rev. 5:8; 6:9-11; 8:3-5). The "bowls of prayer" will be full in heaven before Jesus releases the seven seals of judgment on the earth.

> *8 When He had taken the scroll, the four living creatures and the twenty-four elders fell down before the Lamb, each having a harp, and golden bowls full of incense, which are the prayers of the saints. 9 And they sang a new song, saying: "You are worthy to take the scroll, and to open its seals; for You were slain, and have redeemed us to God by Your blood... (Rev. 5:8-9)*

The new song originates at God's Throne and is dynamically related to Jesus' Coming to earth (Ps. 33:3-14; 40:3-10; 96:1; 98:1; 149:1-9; Rev. 5:8-4; 14:2-3). God promised to establish intercessors who will never be silent until He restores Jerusalem.

> *6 I have set watchmen on your walls...they shall never hold their peace (be silent, NAS) day or night...7 give Him no rest till He establishes...Jerusalem a praise in the earth. (Isa. 62:6-7)*

Isa. 42:10-13 with Rev. 22:17 gives us the clearest picture of the End-Time Church "praying in conjunction with prophetic singing" to invite the Second Coming of Jesus. The prophetic "new song" will be released in all nations leading to Jesus' Second Coming. The End-Time worship movement will be led by prophetic music and songs.

> *10 Sing to the LORD a new song, and His praise from the ends of the earth, you who go down to the sea, and all that is in it, you coastlands and you inhabitants of them! 11 Let the wilderness and its cities lift up their voice, the villages that Kedar inhabits. Let the inhabitants of Sela sing, let them shout from the top of the mountains. 12 Let them give glory to the LORD, and declare His praise in the coastlands. 13 The LORD shall go forth like a mighty man (Jesus' Second Coming); He shall stir up His zeal like a man of war. He shall cry out, yes, shout aloud; He shall prevail against His enemies. 14 "I have held My peace...I have been still and restrained Myself. Now I will cry like a woman in labor, I will pant and gasp at once.15 I will lay waste the mountains and hill (End-Time judgments)..." (Isa. 42:10-15) 16 The Lord will descend from heaven with a shout...and with the trumpet of God...17 We who are alive...shall be caught up together with them in the clouds... (1 Thes. 4:16-17)*

At the end-of-the-age there will be 144,000 prophetic singers from the 5-6 million Jewish intercessors who are described as those who call on God's name in worship and intercession. The 144,000 will stand with Jesus in His government as they sing the new song of the Lord.

> *1 Behold, a Lamb standing on Mount Zion, and with Him 144,000...2 I heard the sound of harpists playing their harps. 3 They sang ...a new song before the Throne...and no one could learn that song except the 144,000 who were redeemed from the earth. (Rev. 14:1-3)*

The End-Time Church will not be raptured before the Great Tribulation. Rather, the praying Church releases the judgments of the Great Tribulation. God's End-Time judgments will be released by the songs of the redeemed. David prophesied that prophetic worship that will release God's End-Time judgments.

> *6 Let the high praises of God be in their mouth...7 to execute vengeance on the nations, and punishments on the peoples; 8 to bind their kings with chains...9 to execute on them the written judgment-- This honor have all His saints. Praise the LORD! (Ps. 149:6-9)*

The Church at the end of the age will see a great worship movement.

> *14 They shall lift up their voice, they shall sing; for the majesty of the LORD they shall cry aloud from the sea. 15 Therefore glorify the LORD in the dawning light, the name of the LORD God of Israel in the coastlands of the sea. 16 From the ends of the earth we have heard songs: (Isa. 24:14-16)*

> *1 In that day this song will be sung in the land of Judah: "We have a strong city; God will appoint salvation for walls and bulwarks. 2 Open the gates, that the righteous nation which keeps the truth may enter in. (Isa. 26:1-2)*

The Great End-Time Conflict: Two Global Worship Movements

The great conflict at the end-of-the-age will be between two Houses of Prayer or between two global worship movements. The Holy Spirit is raising up the most powerful prayer and worship movement in history. It will be the Church's "first line of defense" against the Antichrist's worship movement and his persecutions. The Antichrist will raise up a *state-financed false worship worldwide movement* to hinder the Holy Spirit's worship movement (Rev. 13:4, 8, 12, 15). This worship movement will cause the people in the kingdom of darkness to have a deep heart connect with Satan. The music in this movement will move people emotionally and will be backed up by signs and wonders.

> *8 All who dwell on the earth will worship him (Antichrist), whose names have not been written in the Book of Life of the Lamb slain from the foundation of the world. (Rev. 13:8)*

Satan will use "false prophetic" preaching that will be confirmed with false signs and wonders to raise up his "prophetic" worship and prayer movement.

> *9 The coming of the lawless one (Antichrist) is according to the working of Satan, with all power, signs, and lying wonders, 10 and with all unrighteous deception... (2 Thes. 2:9-10)*
> *24 For false Christ's and false prophets will rise and*

> *show great signs and wonders to deceive, if possible, even the elect. (Mt. 24:24)*

The music and the lyrics will cause the multitudes to weep and be deeply moved so that they will follow the Antichrist even unto death. Angels of light will appear in the massive worship festivals attended by millions. Lucifer was the chief musician in the courts of God before he fell. He knows how to use music powerfully.

> *13 You were in Eden, the garden of God...the workmanship of your timbrels and pipes was prepared for you on the day you were created. 14 You were the anointed cherub...I established you; you were on the holy mountain of God; you walked back and forth in the midst of fiery stones. 15 You were perfect in your ways from the day you were created, till iniquity was found in you...16 Therefore I cast you as a profane thing out of the mountain of God; I destroyed you, O covering cherub, from the midst of the fiery stones. 17 Your heart was lifted up because of your beauty; you corrupted your wisdom for the sake of your splendor; I cast you to the ground...18 You defiled your sanctuaries by the multitude of your iniquities. (Ezek. 28:13-18)*

The Antichrist, the False Prophet and their followers will be fully committed to this false worship movement. Jesus, the Holy Spirit and the End-Time Church will be even more committed to the true worship movement. It is the wisdom of God to give ourselves to this. The False Prophet will perform great signs (plural) that will be great in power as well as great in significance and deception (Rev. 16:14; 19:20; 13:14; Mt. 24:11, 24; Mk. 13:22; 2 Thes. 2:9).

The great miracles will probably often occur in the large Antichrist worship events.

> *12 And he (False Prophet) exercises all the authority of the first beast (Antichrist), and causes the earth... to worship the first beast (Antichrist)...13 He performs great signs, so that he even makes fire come down from heaven on the earth in the sight of men. (Rev. 13:12-13)*

The False Prophet's primary goal is to raise up a worldwide worship movement in which Satan and the Antichrist are worshipped (Rev. 13:4, 8, 12, 15).

> *15 He (False Prophet) was granted power to give breath to the image of the beast...to cause as many as would not worship the image...to be killed. 16 He causes all...rich and poor, free and slave, to receive a mark on their right hand or on their foreheads, 17 and that no one may buy or sell except one who has the mark... (Rev. 13:15-17)*

The False Prophet will call down fire as a counterfeit Elijah who called fire down from heaven in his "clash of power" with the prophets of Baal (1 Kg. 18:38; 2 Kgs. 1:10-12). The False Prophet will have a clash of power with the Two Witnesses who will call fire from heaven (Rev. 11:5). The *image* of the Beast and the *mark* of the Beast will be two components that will mobilize and finance the Antichrist's global worship movement. The *image* of the Beast will mobilize Antichrist's worshippers and penalize those who resist. The *mark* of the Beast will provide economic support for the Antichrist's worship movement and will penalize those who resist. The image of the Beast will be an idol of the Antichrist that will combine cutting edge technology and supernatural demonic elements causing this image to breathe and speak. The image may be like a high-tech hologram that looks and sounds like the Antichrist. I believe that local leaders will have a duplicate image of the Antichrist that will be demonically and technologically connected to the "primary" image in Jerusalem. The result will be a global network of local "Antichrist worship sanctuaries" that may include a hologram of the Antichrist. These demonic local outposts will be the focal points of spiritual warfare as the true houses of prayer fill the earth. The worship that Satan wanted from Jesus is what he demands from the whole earth. Satan offered Jesus the political authority over all the kingdoms of the earth if He would worship him.

> *8 The devil...showed Him all the kingdoms of the world and their glory. 9 And he said to Him, "All these things I will give You if You will fall down and worship me." (Matt. 4:8-9)*

The Antichrist will demand to be worshipped before an idol as Nebuchadnezzar did (Dan. 3:1-6).

> *1 Nebuchadnezzar...made an image of gold, whose height was sixty cubits (90 feet) and its width six cubits (9 feet)...4 Then a herald cried aloud, "...You shall... worship the gold image...6 whoever does not fall down and worship shall be cast into...fiery furnace." (Dan. 3:1-6)*

There will be a great war in the spirit realm over who will be worshipped or who will possess the passion of the human heart. It is a war for our hearts. Michael the Archangel wars with Satan in context to the End-Time worship movement.

> *7 War broke out in heaven: Michael and his angels fought with the dragon...9 So the great dragon was cast out, that serpent of old, called the Devil...he*

> *was cast to the earth, and his angels were cast out*
> *with him. (Rev. 12:7-9)*

It is during this time and within this spiritual climate that God will raise up and glorify his church as a praise in the earth. The Church that becomes a house of prayer will be known for her unceasing and undying devotion in praise and worship to the glorified Christ. These 7 principles to becoming a praying church, if meditated on and implemented in our lives, families, and ministries will prepare us for the greatest drama in human history. It is through the praying church that we will be positioned and prepared for this hour in the earth. It is to this end that our Lord Jesus Christ built his church and it is to this end that we are being restored to the church's original mission and purpose: My house shall be called the House of Prayer for all nations.

The Coming Church of the 21st Century

What will the church, which partners in prayer with Christ in the earth to accomplish this end-time mandate at the end of the age, look like? What will we look like when we repent and return to right pursuits and our purpose as a house of prayer? What will the church look like right before Jesus returns to the earth? The 21st century is going to be the century of the greatest glory of the church in its existence in the earth. This 21st century church is going to be characterized by two main distinctions. It's going to be the century of the church's maturity as the bride of Christ, prepared for her bridegroom, without spot or wrinkle or any such thing, holy and without blemish. And it is going to be the century of the manifestation of the Glory of God. As we come into the second decade of 21st century we are going to see these two characteristics take center stage, the Mature Church as a Bride, and the Glorified Church that manifests the Glory of God in the earth.

Oh what change is going to Transpire in our world as the Church comes to its perfection purpose and state of maturity as the Bride of Christ. This 21st century church is not going to be known by its state of the art buildings, or its religious affiliations, or the size of a particular congregation.

House Churches – My HOME shall be called.....

In the 21st century 5000 to 10,000 member congregations will be as common as storefront churches. But they won't be housed in large elegant illustrious buildings. They will meet in homes and abandoned buildings. Our homes will be called the House of Prayer. The body of believers will be housed in homes throughout a given neighborhood, community, suburb, or city. The outstanding characteristic of this mature perfected church is that its' members will meet in the homes and warehouse-type buildings of their discipleship Pastors throughout the congregation.

> *Act 2:42 And they continued stedfastly in the apostles' doctrine and fellowship, and in breaking of bread, and in prayers. 43 And fear came upon every soul: and many wonders and signs were done by the apostles.*
>
> *44. And all that believed were together, and had all things common; 45. And sold their possessions and goods, and parted them to all men, as every man had need. 46. And they, continuing daily with one accord in the temple, and breaking bread from house to house, did eat their meat with gladness and singleness of heart, 47 Praising God, and having favour with all the people. And the Lord added to the church daily such as should be saved.*

212

Then they will come together within the given city for corporate gatherings of prayer, in some cities daily 3 times a day, or even 24hrs a day, seven days a week, in others cities weekly, or monthly, or even quarterly. In these corporate city-wide gatherings the body of believers will come together in stadiums, or convention centers or large buildings in the city, not for teaching or preaching services but for corporate prayer services, to pray and worship the King of kings and the Lord of lords. The churches of a given city won't be known for its' denominational differences, nor its' doctrinal differences. It won't be known for ministry personalities, nor its' super hero type, one-man show, charismatic televangelists. It won't even be known or stereotyped as a religious establishment.

City & Nation Churches

The church of the 21st century will be known and recognized as a nation. It will be characterized by the city that a body of believers resides in. They will be known as a country, a race, a body of people made up of all nationalities. She will be an amalgamation of every race come together in one body that will be identified, not by skin color, gender or social status, but by the person-hood and relationship of Jesus Christ. They will be the anointed ones, a relational community known by its' love ethic, Loving the Lord with all our Heart, mind soul and strength and our neighbor as ourselves. She will be known by her ability for and responsibility to brotherhood and peace, and to the continual development of succeeding generations preparing them for the unique dynamics of the end-times and the coming kingdom of God in the earth. It will be the redemption of the human race operating in a new order, the kingdom order.

The Mature Perfected Church Can Be Summed Up By the Scriptures in Isaiah 2:1 and Micah 4:1

Micah 4:1-5 *But in the last days it shall come to pass, that the mountain of the house of the Lord shall be established in the top of the mountains, and it shall be exalted above the hills; and people shall flow unto it. And many nations shall come, and say Come let us go up to the mountain of the Lord , and to the house of the God of Jacob; and he will teach us his ways, and we shall walk in his paths: for the law of the Lord (Love the Lord with all thy heart, soul, and mind, and love thy neighbor as thyself) shall go forth of Zion(The Church), and the word of the Lord from Jerusalem.*

And he shall Judge among many people, and rebuke strong nations afar off; and they shall beat their swords into plowshares, and their spears into prunning-hooks: nation shall not lift up sword against nation, neither shall they learn war any more.

But they shall sit every man under his vine and under his fig tree; and none shall make them afraid: for the mouth of the Lord of hosts hath spoken it, for all the people will walk everyone in the name of his God, and we will walk in the name of the Lord our God forever and ever.

The two primary differences in the mature, perfected church which is a bride in Love with her bridegroom coming forth in the 21st century firstly will be:

1. An emphasis of His church on knowing the ways of God, not just the acts of God.
2. It will be an emphasis on walking and dwelling in his paths.

John the Baptist declares concerning the coming kingdom of God in Matthew 3:1-3; Repent ye, for the kingdom of heaven is at hand. For this is he that was spoken of by the prophet Esaias, saying, The voice of one crying in the wilderness, *Prepare ye the way of the Lord and make his paths straight.*

Forerunner messengers will be raised up in this 21st century church that will preach the message of repentance preparing the way of the Lord. They will begin to release the 3 fold revelation of Christ in this 21st century church that will be the revelation of Christ that is seen right before the Lord returns. That 3 fold revelation of Christ will be:

1. **Christ as Bridegroom** – Which will restore the First commandment to first place in His body, releasing the bridal paradigm to the church causing them to Love the Lord God with all their heart, mind, soul and strength.

2. **Christ as King** – Which will restore dominion, power and release a revival of sign, wonders and miracles to earth causing the church to possess with power the earth and those that dwell therein as the spoil from the enemy to our Lord

3. **Christ as Judge** – Which will release justice and a shaking of everything that can be shaken in the

earth. Luke 18:7. This will be a time of great offence and fallen away in the earth and church as the Lord extracts vengeance on the enemies of God and the nations of the earth.

This will be a revelation that messengers will have enabling them to prepare of the way of the Lord. Forerunner messengers will know His ways and will show his ways in the earth.

The 9 Ways of the Lord

In the scriptures there are nine specific references that point to what the ways of the Lord are. They are listed below as:

1. The Way of Salvation– Jo. 14:6; Acts 4:12; 16:17.
2. The Way of Righteousness - II Peter 2:21.
3. The Way of Peace - Romans 3:23.
4. The Way of Truth - II Peter 2:2.
5. The Way of Holiness - Isaiah 35:8,
6. The Way of Excellence (Love)-1 Cor 12:31,
7. The Way of Life - Acts 2:28, Proverbs 6:20-23,
8. The Way of Wisdom - Prov. 4:11
9. The Way of Understanding - Prov. 9:6

Walking in these nine ways will be the primary mark of the 21st century church. This will be what ushers into the earth the glory of the Lord that will cover the earth as the waters cover the seas, where the kingdoms of this world will become the kingdoms of our God and His Christ (His Church-the Anointed ones).

CHAPTER 13

HOW TO DEVELOP A STRONG PRAYER LIFE

We pray always for you that our God would count you worthy of this calling, and fulfill all the good pleasure of His goodness and the work of faith with power... (2 Thes. 1:11)

Without knowledge of how to pray most people will not pray. Without a prayer format many will not pray with any consistency. Therefore I would like to consummate this book on prayer with a chapter on How to develop a strong prayer life, from a very good teaching I heard while at IHOP-KC by Mike Bickle that increased my prayer life seemingly 10-fold. This chapter is aimed at empowering you prayer life with discipline and desire.

Prayer has different expressions such as *intimacy with God* (includes prayer-reading the Word and fellowshipping with the Spirit), *interceding for revival, justice, or social transformation* (also referred to as contending prayer), providing *prayer covering for individuals*, and *praying for the sick*. In this way, we encounter God, do the works of the kingdom, and change the world. A consistent prayer life is essential to the forerunner ministry—only through a lifestyle of prayer can we receive the fullness of what God has provided for us. The forerunner commitment is to seek to spend at least two hours of prayer a day in any of these four expressions. I also encourage forerunners to pray-read through the book of Revelation once a week.

What Is Prayer

What is prayer? It is talking to God. It is at the same time a great privilege, a fierce struggle, and a powerful miracle of the Spirit who helps us in our weakness in prayer. Prayer is so necessary because it causes our spirit to be energized, releases God's blessing on our circumstances, and results in real changes in the Church, the nations, and society. Prayer is a place of abiding in Christ or connecting with the Spirit that energizes us to love God (first commandment) which causes us to overflow in love for others (second commandment).

> ⁵ He who <u>abides</u> in Me...bears <u>much</u> fruit; for without Me you can do <u>nothing</u>. (Jn. 15:5)

Prayer was never meant to be duty-based or merely results-oriented. Rather, it is the place of encounter with God where our spirit is energized as we grow to love Him more. It positions us to be energized to love God and people by receiving God's love as a Father and Bridegroom. We love others better as we encounter God's heart. We do not have to give up our prayer time to make time to minister to people. We can do both. Most of us can seize time for the kingdom from the time we spend on entertainment or in gaining extra money that we may not really need. Prayer that leads to intimacy with God protects our spirit from burnout as we minister to many people over the years. Our prayer life serves as a buffer against spiritual burnout. Maintaining a heart connect with Jesus is the lifeline that enables us for decades to sustain our ministry of winning the lost, healing the sick, and doing works of justice and compassion.

Why does God want us to Pray

Why does God want us to pray? He wants us to connect with His heart in deep partnership. Therefore, asking God for everything is a foundational principle of the kingdom. We must specifically ask, not just think about our need with frustration and desperation.

> [6] *In everything by prayer...let your requests be made known to God... (Phil. 4:6)*

There are blessings that God has chosen to give, but withholds them until we ask Him. In this way, He protects His relationship with us by not answering until we connect with Him by asking.

> [18] *The Lord will wait, that He may be gracious to you...*[19] *He will be very gracious to you at the sound of your cry; when He hears it, He will answer you. (Isa. 30:18-19)*

Practical Issues in Developing a Consistent Prayer Life

Three ways to strengthen our prayer life are to set a *schedule* for regular prayer times, make a *prayer list*, and have a *right view* of God. A schedule establishes *"when"* we will pray. A prayer list gives us focus on *"what"* to pray. A right view of God causes us to *"want"* to pray. While I was attending college, a leader encouraged me to put two simple practices in place that have helped me to sustain my prayer life since that time. The first suggestion he gave me was that I should schedule a time to pray. The second was to create and utilize a prayer list.

Most people will pray ten times more with the simplicity of developing a schedule and prayer lists. Many who love God never develop a consistent prayer life because they lack these. Over the years I have talked with many who refuse to do these two things, considering them to be legalistic, though they confess with pain their inability to sustain their prayer life. Once our prayer time has been scheduled, we must consider some of that time as "sacred time," treating it as a *real appointment with the King*. I committed to the Lord to treat certain scheduled prayer times as sacred appointments that I would not miss except in an emergency. Using a prayer list is an essential tool that helps me focus as I pray. I take liberty to deviate from my prayer list or *omit parts* of it as the "winds of inspiration" touch me.

Developing a Prayer List

When developing a prayer list, it is helpful to understand that there are three main <u>prayer themes</u>.

1). *Gifts* of the Spirit: God's power and favor being released

2). *Fruit* of the Spirit: God's character formed in us or others

3). *Wisdom* of the Spirit: God's mind or the spirit of revelation imparted

We ask for the gifts, fruit, and wisdom of the Spirit to be released in each <u>prayer focus</u>: intimacy, petition, and intercession. We connect with God, receive blessing, and change the world.

Intimacy: Focuses on giving my love and devotion to God. This type of prayer includes worship, meditation on the Word (prayer-reading it), and fellowshipping with the Spirit.

Petition: Asks for God's blessing on my <u>personal life and ministry</u>. We pray for a breakthrough on our <u>inner man</u> (heart), <u>circumstances</u> (physical, financial, relational), and <u>ministry</u> that God's power would be released through our hands, words, and deeds.

Intercession: Asks for God's power or justice <u>for others</u> (people, places, strategic issues).

Prayer for people and places: Individuals in ministries, marketplace and government, and for the destiny of ministries, cities, or nations (YWAM, Jerusalem, Egypt, etc.)

Prayer for strategic issues in society: Government (elections, abortion), oppression (human trafficking, abortion), natural disasters (hurricanes, droughts), diseases, etc.

Right View of God: Tender Father and Passionate Bridegroom

Foundational to our life of prayer is cultivating a right view of God. Many have a wrong view of God that sees Him as an angry taskmaster forcing us to endure conversation (prayer) with Him to prove our devotion to Him. As we perceive God as our tender Father and Jesus as our passionate Bridegroom king, we will be energized in our spirit to confidently seek Him with all of our heart. Encountering the father heart of God is foundational to growing in prayer. Jesus prayed for us that we might know that the Father loves us as He loves Jesus, thus giving us great worth.

> [23] *That the world may know that You...have loved them <u>as</u> You have loved Me. (Jn. 17:23)*

We can have the assurance that we are enjoyed by God the Father, even in our weakness (Ps. 18:19, 35; 130:3-4). We pray very differently when our spirit is confident before God with assurance that He enjoys us. The Father is filled with <u>tender mercy</u>. He is gentle with our weakness after we repent. We have "received the Spirit of adoption by whom we cry out, 'Abba, Father.'" In Hebrew, *abba* is a term of endearment, much like *papa* in our culture.

> ¹⁵ *You received the <u>Spirit of adoption</u> by whom we cry out, "<u>Abba, Father</u>." (Rom. 8:15)*

Understanding Jesus as our Bridegroom and ourselves as His cherished Bride equips us to have a vibrant prayer life (Eph. 5:29-32). Many view Jesus as mostly mad or mostly sad, but He has a heart filled with <u>gladness</u> (Heb. 1:9) and <u>fiery affections</u> in His jealous love for us. As sons of God, we are in the position to experience *God's throne* as heirs of His power (Rev. 3:21; Rom. 8:17). As the Bride, we are in the position to experience *God's heart* (affections).

How to Meditate On the Word: Pray-Reading the Word

The most substantial way in which we can bolster our prayer lives is by feeding on the Word of God. This includes engaging in active conversation with God as we read His Word. Scripture gives us the "conversational material" in our prayer life. This way makes prayer more enjoyable.

> ⁸ *This Book of the Law shall not depart from your mouth, but you shall <u>meditate in it day and night</u>...then you will make your way <u>prosperous</u>, and...will have <u>good success</u>. (Josh. 1:8)*

Bible study must lead to dialogue with God. Jesus rebuked the Pharisees, saying, "You search the Scriptures without using them to develop a real relationship with God (Jn. 5:39-40).

> *[39] You search the Scriptures, for in them you think you have...life; these are they which <u>testify of Me</u>. [40] You are not willing to <u>come to Me</u> (dialogue) that you may have <u>life</u>. (Jn. 5:39-40)*

Two broad categories of truth related to pray-reading the Word (meditating on Scripture) are: Scriptures that focus on promises "*to believe*" and Scriptures that exhort us "*to obey*."

We actively dialogue with God by praying promises that we are "*to believe*" from His Word. First, *we <u>thank</u> God* for a particular truth. We turn that truth into <u>declarations</u> of thanksgiving or trust. For example, we say, "Thank you that You love, forgive, lead, and provide for me."Second, *we <u>ask</u> God to reveal* particular truths to us (Eph. 1:17). For example, pray, "Father, reveal to me more of Your love, forgiveness, direction, and provision for me."

We actively dialogue with God by praying truths back to Him that exhort us "*to obey*" His Word. First, *we <u>commit</u> ourselves to obey God* in the specific way set forth in a passage. We make <u>declarations of our resolve</u> to obey, saying, "I set my heart to obey in speech, time, and money." Second, *we <u>ask</u> God to empower us to obey* a particular truth. We <u>ask God for help</u> to give us wisdom, motivation, and power to obey in specific areas. For example pray: "Father help me to love You, to bridle my speech, or use my time and money in full obedience." We must articulate our love, gratitude, and requests to Jesus in simple phrases. Take time to *journal* or record your thoughts and prayers as you "pray-read" through Scripture. This helps us capture the truths that the Spirit gives us and to develop language to talk with God.

> *[2] <u>Take words with you</u>, and return to the LORD. <u>Say to Him</u>, "Take away all iniquity; receive us graciously, for we will offer the sacrifices of our lips. (Hos. 14:2)*

In prayer and meditation, we speak to God <u>on His throne</u> and to God the Spirit, who <u>dwells in our spirit</u>. If we will talk to the Spirit, then we will walk in the Spirit and receive His work in us. Ask the Spirit to let you "see what He sees and feel what He feels" about your life and others.

> [14] *...The love of God, and the <u>fellowship of the Holy Spirit</u> be with you all. (2 Cor. 13:14, NAS)*

Take time to linger in His presence. Speak *affectionately* by intermittently saying, "I love You." Speak *slowly* and *softly* (not shouting or preaching at the indwelling Spirit), *briefly* (short phrases not paragraphs), and *minimally* (listen more than talk) with many *pauses* and *silence*.

The Foundation of Justice: Night And Day Prayer

The Mystery of Intercession involves speaking God's Word back to Him concerning a person, city, or nation. We tell God what He tells us to tell Him as the means of releasing His power. The mystery is that intercession is so simple and weak and thus, accessible to every all.

> [27] *God has chosen the [so called] <u>weak things</u> of the world to put to shame the things which are mighty...*[29] *that no flesh should glory... (1 Cor. 1:27-29)*

The majesty of intercession is seen in that Jesus rules through intercession (Ps. 2:9).

> [25] *<u>He always (forever) lives to make intercession</u> for them. (Heb. 7:25)*

In Genesis 1, Jesus spoke forth the plans of the Father's heart to release the power of the Spirit. The Father had many plans for the earth, and the Spirit was present, yet the earth remained dark, formless, and void until Jesus spoke the word to release the Spirit's power (Gen. 1:2-11; Ps. 33:6, 9; Jn. 1:3; Eph. 3:9; Col. 1:16). Jesus functioned in a form of intercession in Genesis 1. Jesus upholds or sustains the created order by speaking the Word (a type of intercession).

> [3] Who (Jesus)...upholding all things by the word of His power... (Heb. 1:3)

Each time we say what God says, it marks us and changes us. This process progressively renews us. I compare it to a computer programmer who rewrites thousands of lines of code when developing a computer program. God's words are *spirit and life* and they impart life to us. When we say what God says, we receive impartation that illuminates our mind and tenderizes our heart.

> [63] The words that I [Jesus] speak to you are *spirit*, and they are *life*. (Jn. 6:63)

Ten Prayers to Receive Strength in the Inner Man:

F-E-L-L-O-W-S-H-I-P

> [16] TO BE STRENGTHENED WITH MIGHT THROUGH HIS SPIRIT IN THE INNER MAN... (EPH. 3:16)

F- Fear of God: Father, release the spirit of the fear of God into my heart. Release the lightning and thunder from Your Throne (Rev. 4:5) to strike my heart with Your majesty. Release holy dread on my heart that makes me tremble before You. Unite my heart to Your heart and Word.

> [11] *Unite my heart (to Your heart and Word) to fear Your name. (Ps. 86:11)*

E- Endurance (perseverance, patience): Father, strengthen my spirit with endurance that I may do Your will with zeal (diligence) and that I not quit in my fervent pursuit of You and Your will.

> [11] *Being strengthened with all power...may have great endurance and patience... (Col. 1:11 NIV)*

L- Love: Father, pour out Your love into my heart by releasing the influences of the Spirit to give me revelation of Your love for me, that it may overflow in love back to Jesus and to others. (The anointing to love God is our greatest goal, possession, and reward in this age).

> [9] *I pray, that your love may abound still more...in knowledge and all discernment. (Phil. 1:9)*

L- Light of glory: Father, let me see the light of Your glory (or encounter the glory realm). Give me Holy Spirit encounters (dreams, visions, angelic visitations, manifestations of light, fire, wind) as You gave to Moses, Isaiah, Ezekiel, and John (Ex. 33-34:29-30; Isa. 6; Ezek. 1; Rev. 1).

> [6] *A great light from heaven shone around me...* [8] *He said to me, "I am Jesus of Nazareth..."* [11] *I could not see for the glory of that light...I came to Damascus. (Acts 22:6-11)*

> [18] *And he (Moses) said, "Please, show me Your glory." (Ex. 33:18)*

> [6] *Lord, lift up the light of Your countenance upon us. (Ps. 4:6)*

O- One thing life focus: Father, I choose to be a person of one thing who often sits at Your feet. I set my heart to spend <u>quality time</u> with You and to cultivate an <u>inward gaze</u> toward You. <u>*Alert*</u> me when I lose this focus, <u>*align*</u> my life circumstances so I can walk this out and <u>*anoint*</u> my times with You that I may feel Your love and feel desire for You and Your Word.

> [4] <u>*One thing*</u> *I have desired...*<u>*all the days*</u> *of my life, to* <u>*behold the beauty*</u> *of the Lord. (Ps. 27:4)*

> [42] *But* <u>*one thing*</u> *is needed, and Mary has* <u>*chosen*</u> *that good part... (Lk. 10:42)*

The Word is to create a <u>living active dialogue</u> in our heart with God. We <u>pray-read the Word</u> or converse with Jesus as we read it. To love God with all our mind involves taking time to fill our heart with God's word. We gain revelation of God by meditating on it.

We gain the "fuel of intimacy" in times of prayer by connecting and relating to God as a person. This empowers us to love God and man. This is the key to not burning out. David set his heart to consistently set the Lord before him as a lifestyle.

> [8] *I have* <u>*set the Lord always*</u> *before me... (Ps. 16:8)*

W- Count me worthy (faithfulness unto fullness): Strengthen me to <u>walk in such faithfulness </u>that You consider me worthy to walk in my highest calling in this age and the age to come. We need God's help to see and gain victory over the blind spots in our life that we are not focused on.

> [11] *We* <u>*pray always*</u> *for you that our God would* <u>*count you worthy*</u> *of this calling, and* <u>*fulfill all*</u> *the good pleasure of His goodness and the work of faith with power... (2 Thes. 1:11)*

No one is "worthy" to receive forgiveness. It is a free gift because of Jesus' worthiness. Rather, we are to have a *worthy response* to God by living free of compromise, thus we are prepared or are found <u>worthy to walk in the fullness</u> of our calling.

> *²³ May the God of peace <u>sanctify you completely;</u> may your spirit, soul, and body be <u>preserved blameless</u> (without compromise) at the coming of our Lord... (1 Thes. 5:23)*

> *¹³ That He may <u>establish your hearts blameless</u> in holiness before God... (1 Thes. 3:13)*

> *¹ I have made a <u>covenant with my eyes</u>; why should I look on a woman? (Job 31:1)*

S- *Speech*: Father, set a guard over my lips. Free me from defensive, angry, and foolish speech (Eph. 4:29; 5:4). Sustained communion with God requires restrained conversation with man. The Spirit is quenched in us by unwholesome speech: filthy, foolish, coarse jesting (Eph. 4:29-5:4)

> *³ <u>Set a guard</u>, O LORD, over my mouth; <u>keep watch</u> over the door of my lips. (Ps. 141:3)*

> *¹⁴ Let the <u>words of my mouth</u> and the meditation of my heart <u>be acceptable</u>... (Ps. 19:14)*

H- *Humility*: Jesus, I want to learn from You how to walk in lowliness. I commit to take Your yoke of humility (lowliness of heart) on my life in my attitudes, speech, and actions.

> *²⁹ Take My yoke...and <u>learn</u> from Me, for I am gentle and <u>lowly in heart</u>... (Mt. 11:29)*

My House shall be Called the House of Prayer

I- Insight unto intimacy (wisdom): Father give me insight into Your Word, will, and ways. Give me wisdom that I may <u>walk with You</u> in intimacy under the Spirit's creative leadership. I want to partner together with You in every issue in my life including my finances, schedule, emotions, fears, addictions, circumstances, physical body (diet, health), relationships (in the home, office, ministry), my future, etc. Give me new ideas in each area of my life.

> [17] *May give to you the spirit of <u>wisdom</u> and <u>revelation</u> in the knowledge of Him... (Eph. 1:17)*

> [9] *Ask that you may be <u>filled with the knowledge of His will</u> in all wisdom and spiritual understanding;* [10] *that you may have a walk worthy of the Lord... (Col. 1:9-10)*

> [26] *The Holy Spirit...will <u>teach you all things</u>... (Jn. 14:26)*

P- Peace and Joy: Father, strengthen my heart with supernatural peace and joy that overpowers fear, anxiety, phobias and addictions. Sin grows fastest when fear and anxiety are present in us.

> [7] *The <u>peace of God</u>...will <u>guard your hearts</u> and minds through Christ Jesus. (Phil. 4:7)*

> [13] *Now may the God of hope <u>fill</u> you with <u>all joy and peace</u> in believing, that you may <u>abound in hope</u> (confidence) by the <u>power</u> of the Holy Spirit. (Rom. 15:13)*

My House shall be Called the House of Prayer

CHAPTER 14

HOW TO ORGANIZE CORPORATE INTERCESSION IN THE HOUSE OF PRAYER

And when they had prayed, the place where they were assembled together was shaken; and they were all filled with the Holy Spirit, and they spoke the word of God with boldness." (Acts 4:24-31)

What is intercession? Intercession is intimate partnership and agreement with God.

1. Intercession is intimacy. Prayer is an exchange of romance. God speaks to us and it moves our hearts. When we speak back to God, His heart is moved. God desires to establish or deepen this romantic relationship with us. He desires intimacy with us. He wants us to know His heart and more so, to feel the very emotions of His heart, and then He wants to hear us cry out for the longings of His heart to come to pass. His longings become our longings. It's partnership at the most intimate level possible.

We begin to feel and do what God feels and does. *"For Zion's sake I WILL NOT HOLD MY PEACE, and for Jerusalem's sake I WILL NOT REST…"(Isaiah 62:1)"I have set watchmen on your walls, O Jerusalem; THEY SHALL NEVER HOLD THEIR PEACE day or night. You who make mention of the Lord, do not keep silent, and GIVE HIM NO REST…"(Isaiah 62:6)*

2. Intercession is partnership. Intercession is the means by which God's will is established on earth. God does not act apart from human beings partnering with His heart. Intercession expresses

the bridal identity of the church. There is nothing more powerful that can fuel God's heart to move upon the earth than the cry of His bride, whose desires reflect His own.

3. Intercession is agreement with God. Intercession is agreement with what God promised to do. When we ask God to do what He desires to do, we are declaring that we agree that His desires are good, and that His desires have become our desires.

Intercession Expresses God's Definition of the Church

"...My house shall be called a HOUSE OF PRAYER for all nations."(Isaiah 56:7)

"...PRAYER ALSO WILL BE MADE FOR HIM (JESUS) CONTINUALLY, and daily
He shall be praised."(Psalm 72:15)

"PRAY WITHOUT CEASING..."(1 Thessalonians 5:17)

What Do I Do During an Intercession Set

1. Experience enjoyable prayer. *Experiencing God's beauty and God's burning desire for us is what makes prayer enjoyable.* Experiencing God's beauty and desire is the primary source of power that will fuel the End Time prayer movement. The power to engage in night and day prayer is found in having a heart that enjoys God. Encountering God's beauty and desire for us is where we most enjoy our primary reward, which is God Himself. Our primary reward is not the breakthrough of revival. Revival is fantastic, but it is our secondary reward. Jesus Himself is our primary reward. We carry this reward inside our hearts. In other words, we live with a fascinated heart as we drink deeply of God's beauty and desire for us.

2.   Experience God's beauty. This means to understand and experience revelation of the attributes of God as given by the Holy Spirit. This leads to an elation of our spirit, which can be felt in our emotions and which transforms the way that we think and feel about God, ourselves and others.

How Do we Experience God's Beauty

1. Simply ask God to reveal His beauty to you.
"PLEASE, SHOW ME YOUR GLORY."(Exodus 33:18) "That the Father of Glory would GIVE TO YOU A SPIRIT OF WISDOM AND REVELATION IN THE KNOWLEDGE OF HIM (JESUS), THE EYES OF YOUR UNDERSTANDING BEING ENLIGHTENED, that you may know what is the hope of His calling, what are the riches of His inheritance in the saints, and what is the exceeding greatness of His power toward us..."(Ephesians 1:17-19)

2. Read the Word, turning it into dialogue with God.
 The Bible is the Living Word of God, Jesus Christ. When we dialogue with God about His Word, we invite Him to tell us about who He is and we open our hearts to the very nature and therefore, beauty, of God.

3. Pray in the Spirit and sing spontaneously.

4. Our personal prayer language edifies us by renewing our inner man, or, charging our "spiritual battery." It tenderizes our spirit with the knowledge of God. Praying in the Spirit makes us sensitive to small fragments of divine information. The Lord imparts divine information about who He is and how to pray.

5. The way the Bride prepares for war is that she engages with the Holy Spirit through speaking in tongues. When we speak in

tongues, our heart becomes connected with God's heart in an exchange of love between Him and us. Tongues open the human spirit to God as we focus on the Father's Throne with a heart cry of "I love you" to Jesus.

Sing Spontaneously.

1. Singing spontaneously releases both the faith and intensity to encounter the manifest presence of God. This opens the human spirit to the Holy Spirit in an enhanced way.

2. There are two ways to sing spontaneously:

a. Singing with our spirit in tongues. The human spirit both prays and sings.

b. Singing with our understanding from the Scripture. The human mind both prays and sings. *I will SING WITH THE SPIRIT, and I will also SING WITH THE UNDERSTANDING."*

(1 Cor. 14:14-15) "Let the word of Christ dwell in you richly in all wisdom, teaching and admonishing one another IN PSALMS AND HYMNS AND SPIRITUAL SONGS, SINGING WITH GRACE IN YOUR HEARTS TO THE LORD."(Col. 3:16)"Speaking to one another in psalms and hymns and spiritual songs, SINGING AND MAKING MELODY IN YOUR HEART TO THE LORD."(Eph. 5:19)

The Benefits of Praying and Singing In Tongues:

1. It is a universal benefit. It is not just reserved for those with a special calling.

2. It is easy to operate in tongues. It does not require special training.

3. It is a free gift to all without the need to earn anything, therefore, there is no pride of attainment.

4. It unifies intercessors instead of isolating them in individual prayer.

5. It inspires our spirit rather than leaving us with spiritual dullness before God.

6. It focuses our spirit on God rather than requiring the need for constant creative language.

7. It has a deep impact reaching the inner man and not just our intellect.

8. It expands our capacity in the Lord. In other words, when our spirit is engaged, our mind can still receive from God and others.

9. It gives us the ability to continue long hours in prayer without being limited by our human language and affection.

10. It is a springboard into other spiritual gifts.

Experience God's Desire.

This means to understand and sense, or feel, what God wants do in us, in others and in the events of human history on the earth and into eternity. When the Holy Spirit reveals this information to us, we can actually feel the emotions of God's heart inside of us. It is an exhilarating sensation that energizes and frees us from wrong mindsets.

How Do We Experience God's Desire

Pray the prayers of Scripture. Prayer that comes from God's heart expresses His desires. This is the kind of prayer that the Holy Spirit releases Divine authority on.

This is the kind of prayer that God answers. Praying the prayers that come from God's heart enhances the enjoyment of our intimacy with Jesus. Apostolic prayers are prayers that the apostles prayed. The chief apostle is Jesus, and the 12 apostles have prayers recorded in the New Testament. These apostolic prayers are God's very prayers, or desires.

Practice Praying Positive Prayers: When we pray positive prayers, we enter   into the delight of asking for the things that bring pleasure to God. This is a gateway into feeling His desire in our inner man. New Testament Biblical prayers focus on releasing God's grace instead of hindering or removing negative realities like sin or demons. There is a positive focus on the impartation of good instead of a negative focus on removing the realities of sin. The New Testament focus usually flows along themes of joy, thankfulness and victory.

* We do incorporate the negative dimensions of prayer that target confessing, resisting and renouncing the realities of the world, flesh and devil. However, we recognize that they are not the major focus of the New Testament model of praying.

Practical tips for Praying Positive Prayers:

Pray to God instead of talking to people when you pray corporately. Focus on "asking" instead of "explaining." Speak directly to God – be more conscious that He is watching and listening than that others are watching and listening. This will prompt you to direct your heart toward *Him* in love and partnership. Lift specific promises of Scripture up to God and ask for their fulfillment in our present day context.

Ask for the in breaking of positive things rather than the removal of negative things. Example: Positive Prayer: *"Father, I ask that Your light and truth would break in upon the church in Kansas City!"* Negative Prayer: *"Father, I ask that You would remove darkness and deception from the church in Kansas City!"*Note: God hears, cares about and discerns all prayer, whether positive or negative. Because of our natural human tendency to become weary and discouraged, praying positive prayer allows us to maintain prayer day in and day out by helping us engage in joyful supplication rather than trying to bear the emotional weight of negative realities expressed through negative prayer. This is especially relevant in a 24-7 prayer ministry such as IHOP-KC. It is because of both the Biblical model and human dynamics that we encourage positive prayer.*

Prayer on the Microphone

Everyone is welcomed and encouraged to pray on the microphone. Praying on the microphone is in no way mandated, but encouraged as a way to engage your heart in intercession and to help lead the prayer meeting. Anyone can do this, no matter what their personality, style, or disposition.

A Few Helpful Tips for Praying on the Microphone

a. If you wish to pray on the microphone, make your way to the front row of blue chairs. They usually fill up quickly. Be prepared to wait at least 45 minutes for your turn since the prayer meeting is intermingled with worship and other prayer focuses.

b. Select a New Testament prayer or Old Testament prophetic decree to pray out of. The "key apostolic prayers" list is a great place to start.

c. Please hold the microphone VERY close to your mouth (to prevent sound feedback in the room). Don't feel any pressure to shout on the microphone, rather speak at a moderate volume level.

d. You have the option to pray with the singers or not. If you pause, the   singers on the platform will begin singing spontaneous prayers. Within every 2-3 short songs, you may interject more short prayerful phases. In this way, we are going back and forth in team ministry in intercession.

e. Pray "positive prayers." (See *"practical tips for praying positive prayer," page*)

f. When you are finished, feel free to simply set the microphone down and walk away.

How to Pray Using the Apostolic Prayers or Old Testament Prophetic Decrees in the Harp and Bowl Model:

a. Decide what or who the target of your prayer is examples: The church in Columbus Ohio, the church in any city or nation, the government of a country, the lost of any city or nation, etc.

b. Using the "Key Apostolic Prayers" List (Page 23-24) or "Prophetic Decrees and Promises from OT Prophets" List (Harp and Bowl Syllabus, part 2, page 142-145), pick the prayer or decree that best expresses what you want to pray for.
Example #1: If you want to pray that the church in Kansas City would grow in the knowledge of Jesus, you might pick *Apostolic Prayer #1: "THAT THE GOD OF OUR LORD JESUS CHRIST, THE*

FATHER OF GLORY MAY GIVE TO YOU THE SPIRIT OF WISDOM AND REVELATION IN THE KNOWLEDGE OF HIM, the eyes of your understanding being enlightened, that you may know what is the hope of His calling, what are the riches of the glory of His inheritance in the saints, and what is the exceeding greatness of His power toward us who believe, according to the working of His mighty power." (Ephesians 1:17-19)

Example #2: If you want to pray that the church in Kansas City would experience revival, you might pick the *Prophetic Promise* found in Isaiah 35:1-2: *"The wilderness and the wasteland shall be glad for them, and THE DESERT SHALL REJOICE AND BLOSSOM AS THE ROSE; IT SHALL BLOSSOMABUNDANTLY AND REJOICE, EVEN WITH JOY AND SINGING..."(Isaiah 35:1-2)*

1. No matter what you want to pray for, you should be able to find an Apostolic Prayer or a Prophetic promise to match the cry of your heart – they cover pretty much everything. Feel free to ask the associate prayer leader to help you find an Apostolic Prayer or Prophetic promise that matches the burden of your heart.

2. It's okay if you don't feel anything "burning" in your heart. If you don't feel something specific that you want to pray for, just pick any prayer or promise – all of these prayers and promises are on God's heart all of the time, so it's impossible to pray the wrong prayer!

3. You can choose to pray through just a phrase or a section of the Apostolic Prayer or Prophetic promise. You don't have to pray through the whole prayer/promise.

If helpful, create an outline of the prayer. This may help you to organize your thoughts and therefore present a clear train of thought for others to follow as you lead the room in intercession. Pick 2-3 points (actual phrases from the Apostolic Prayer or Prophetic promise) to pray through. Your prayer will be more focused if you concentrate on a few points of the prayer, rather than trying to pray through all of the points and themes of the prayer.

Example: Ephesians 1:17-19:
Point #1: *"That the Father of Glory may give to you the spirit of wisdom and revelation in the knowledge of Him"* Point #2: *"The eyes of your understanding being enlightened"* Point #3: *"That you may know what is the hope of His calling"*

Example: Isaiah 35:1-2:
Point #1: *"The desert shall rejoice"*
Point #2: *"the desert shall blossom abundantly"*
Point #3: *"Even with joy and singing"*

4. Make notes under each of your main points as you prepare to pray. Include cross-references and your own expression of the Biblical prayer or promise.

5. Pray through each of your points, one at a time, either pausing to let the singers sing or not. Practice articulating your heart.

Why Is It Important To Articulate Our Hearts

It is exhilarating to develop language to express the truth that God deposits in our hearts through His Word. We feel the sensation of pleasure in our heart when we express God's truth through our own understanding and with our own vocabulary. Human Beings are the only creatures on earth who are given the gift of language. It is an awesome and fascinating privilege to be able to communicate the depths of our heart to each other and to God. By developing an ability to put the ideas and feelings that

are in our hearts into words, we do a couple of things:
a. We explore the emotions of God's heart more deeply.
b. We inspire others to identify stirrings in their hearts.
c. We expand our own understanding of the Word of God.

How to Articulate Your Heart

a. Practice putting passages of Scripture into your own words. Example: *"That the eyes of your understanding would be enlightened." "That the innermost part of your spirit would be illuminated" "That your innermost man would be awakened by the light of God" "That the eyes of your heart would fully comprehend"*

b. Cross-referencing is another wonderful tool – finding other Bible verses that explain or expound upon your point to articulate yourself. How good it is to use the Bible to expound on the Bible!

c. It may be helpful to use a thesaurus to expand your vocabulary when meditating on the apostolic prayers.

How to Lead Others in Intercession

When you pray on the microphone, you are helping to *lead* a prayer meeting. When prayer leading or praying on the microphone, the goal is to *serve* the room. The following are IHOP-KC Values that are important to remember when praying on the microphone:

1. Team ministry – we go farther together;
2. Inclusiveness – everyone can participate;
3. The centrality of the Scripture – God's language unifies our heart with His and others.

The following are some dynamics to keep in mind when you are praying on the microphone.

1. Volume – Though it is necessary to hold the microphone very close to your mouth and to speak clearly, *there is no need to shout on the microphone*. A moderate volume level is encouraged, with an occasional projection or shouting volume. The room is not engaged by continual shouting, but rather by dramatic contrasts. Theologically, shouting does not mean that we are more gripped with the Holy Spirit or that we are making a greater impact in the spiritual realm. Authority is not manifested by volume, but by Divine activity.

2. Clarity – This means that it is clear to the room what your prayer focus. Your main points are clearly defined and prayed through and they follow each other in a logical way. Repeating key phrases and using concise statements creates clarity.

3. Topic – Is your prayer focus one that the majority will be eager excited to partner with you on? Praying for the church in Kansas City, or the government of our nation, etc., are examples of focal points that the majority can join with you in. Praying for a friend or relative that no one knows except you may cause disinterest and disengagement of others. Again, we pray on the microphone to lead and serve the room in intercession. Praying on the microphone does not make our prayer any more important to God; rather, it is a tool that helps us join together in prayer.

4. Enthusiasm – Are you passionate about your prayer? Does it show? Others will be more inclined to join in with your prayer if they sense that your heart is engaged and burning.

This does not mean shouting or exaggerating your emotions. This means being aware that you are being heard by others and that you are trying to bring them along with you in intercession. Monotone speech or a casual delivery may cause others to disengage. Remember that you are speaking to God –connect with Him and your passion will be expressed.

5. Length of Prayer – 5 minutes is a pretty good length. If you go longer than 5-7 minutes, often the room will lose interest and disengage. Also, there are usually others waiting to pray after you.

6. Timing– You may want to add little 2-3 second phrases *in between* the singers' singing – not during their singing – to reiterate your point to the room. *Please do not shout over the choruses.* Also, it is helpful to read the room in terms of when to begin warring in the spirit. Usually it is best to go into a time of warring in the spirit when the music and the singers are the most intense-sounding.

There are more dynamics to be aware of when praying on the microphone, but these are the main ones. It will take time to learn to lead the room, but the more you go up there and pray, the more you will learn, the easier it will become and the more enjoyable it will be.

Rapid Fire Prayer

What is rapid fire prayer? Rapid Fire Prayer is a series of short prayers, prayed on the microphone one after the other, interspersed by choruses from the prophetic singers.

Why do we do it? Rapid Fire Prayer provides an opportunity for more people to pray on the microphone per intercession set and it also can bring energy to a prayer meeting because of the energizing dynamic of the short "bursts of prayer" from several different voices. How does a rapid fire prayer cycle work? The prayer leader will announce a rapid fire cycle. He or she will announce what the prayer focus is and will invite 10 – 15 people (anyone who wants to) to come up and *pray a ten to fifteen second prayer* on the microphone. The Rapid Fire cycle leader will start by praying a one or two minute prayer. After that prayer, the singers will sing a chorus. Then one by one, those in line will pray a ten to fifteen second prayer. In between every few intercessors' prayers, the singers will sing a chorus. Then, the next person will pray and so on until everyone in line has prayed. Rapid fire prayer is a great way to begin praying on the microphone if you are nervous or just want to get a "feel" for it.

Small Group Prayer

What is small group prayer? Small group prayer is the gathering together of a small number of people to pray for a particular people group, nation, event, etc.

Why do we do it? Small group prayer is an opportunity to connect our heart with others as we agree together in prayer. This connectivity strengthens us in community and love for one another and also gives us energy in continuing in prayer.

How does small group prayer work? The prayer leader will announce a small group prayer time. He or she will invite anyone so desiring to gather into small groups of 4-5, all over the room, to engage in prayer over any burden the group would like to intercede for together. Do not wait to be invited into a group; simply approach and join a group.

The Life Line

1. What is the "Life Line?" The "Life Line" is made up of strips of red tape along the floor in the front right area of the Prayer Room. "Life Line" offers an opportunity to take a purposed stand in the Prayer Room on the issue of life. It is a means to appeal to heaven for the establishing of a culture of life – and specifically, the ending of abortion – in our nation and the world.

2. Why do we do it? We want to take a determined stance in our plea for life. The "Life Line" is a way to sustain our prayerful appeal for life. It can provide the awareness, focus and energy needed to intercede for this particular issue in an on-going way.

3. How does "Life Line" work? Anyone at any time may take their stand on the "Life Line." Simply come and stand on the red tape and pray for the establishing of life. Meditate on the Word as you pray.

Key Apostolic Intercessory Prayers

1. Prayer for revelation of Jesus' beauty and the Bride's destiny unto transforming our heart

"...the Father of glory, may give to you the SPIRIT OF WISDOM AND REVELATION IN THE KNOWLEDGE OF HIM, the eyes of your understanding being enlightened; that you may know what is the HOPE OF HIS CALLING, what are the riches of the GLORY OF HIS INHERITANCE IN THE SAINTS, and what is the exceeding GREATNESS OF HIS POWER TOWARD US" (Eph. 1:17-19).

2. Prayer for the release of supernatural strength in the heart unto experiencing God's emotions.

"...that He would grant you, according to the riches of His glory, TO BE STRENGTHENED WITH MIGHT THROUGH HIS SPIRIT IN THE INNER MAN, that Christ may dwell in your hearts through faith; that you, being rooted and grounded in love, MAY BE ABLE TO COMPREHEND with all the saints what is the width and length and depth and height-- to know the love of Christ which passes knowledge; that you may be filled with all the fullness of God." *(Eph. 3:16-19)*

3. Prayer for God's love to abound in our heart resulting in

discernment and righteousness.

"And this I pray, that YOUR LOVE MAY ABOUND still more and more in knowledge and all discernment, that you may APPROVE THE THINGS THAT ARE EXCELLENT, that you may be sincere and without offense till the day of Christ, being FILLED WITH THE FRUITS OF RIGHTEOUSNESS which are by Jesus Christ, to the glory and praise of God." (Phil. 1:9-11)

4. Prayer to know God's will, to be fruitful in ministry and strengthened by intimacy with God.

"We...do not cease to pray for you, and to ask that you may be filled with the KNOWLEDGE OF HIS WILL in all wisdom and spiritual understanding; that you may have a WALK WORTHY OF THE LORD, fully pleasing Him, BEING FRUITFUL in every good work and increasing in the knowledge of God; STRENGTHENED WITH ALL MIGHT, according to His glorious power, for all patience and longsuffering with joy; giving thanks to the Father who has qualified us to be partakers of the inheritance
of the saints in the light." (Col. 1:9-12)

5. Prayer for unity within the church across a city.

"Now may the God of patience and comfort GRANT YOU TO BE LIKE-MINDED toward one another, according to Christ Jesus, THAT YOU MAY WITH ONE MIND AND ONE MOUTH glorify the God and Father of our Lord Jesus." (Rom. 15:5-7)

6. Prayer to be filled with supernatural joy, peace and hope.

"Now may the God of hope FILL YOU WITH ALL JOY AND PEACE IN BELIEVING, THAT YOU MAY ABOUND IN HOPE by the power of the Holy Spirit." (Rom. 15:13)

7. Prayer for Israel to be saved through Jesus.

"My heart's desire and prayer to God for ISRAEL is that they may be saved." (Rom. 10:1).

8. Prayer to enriched with the supernatural gifts of the Holy Spirit leading unto righteousness.

"I thank my God always concerning you for the grace of God which was given to you by Christ Jesus, THAT YOU WERE ENRICHED IN EVERYTHING by Him in all utterance and all knowledge, even as the testimony of Christ was confirmed in you, so THAT YOU COME SHORT IN NO GIFT, eagerly waiting for the revelation of our Lord Jesus Christ, who will also confirm you to the end, THAT YOU MAY BE BLAMELESS in the day of our Lord Jesus Christ." (1 Cor. 1:4-8)

9. Prayer for the release of apostolic ministry and to abound in love and holiness

"...we rejoice for your sake before our God, night and day praying exceedingly THAT WE MAY SEE YOUR FACE and PERFECT WHAT IS LACKING in your faith? Now may our God and Father Himself, and our Lord Jesus Christ, DIRECT OUR WAY TO YOU. And may the Lord make you increase and ABOUND IN LOVE to one another and to all...so that He may ESTABLISH YOUR HEARTS BLAMELESS IN HOLINESS before our God and Father at the coming of our Lord Jesus Christ with all His saints." (1 Thes. 3:9-13)

10. Prayer to be equipped and prepared to receive the fullness of God destiny for the church.

"Therefore we also pray always for you THAT OUR GOD WOULD COUNT YOU WORTHY OF THIS CALLING, AND FULFILL ALL THE GOOD PLEASURE OF HIS GOODNESS AND THE WORK OF FAITH WITH POWER, that the name of our Lord Jesus Christ may be glorified in you, and you in Him, according to the grace of our God

and the Lord Jesus Christ." (2 Thes. 1:11-12)
11. Prayer for the Word to increase by the release of Holy Spirit power.

"Finally, brethren, pray for us, THAT THE WORD OF THE LORD MAY RUN SWIFTLY AND BE GLORIFIED, just as it is with you, and that we may be delivered from unreasonable and wicked men; for not all have faith. But the Lord is faithful, who will establish you and guard you from the evil one. And we have confidence in the Lord concerning you, both that you do and will do the things we command you.

NOW MAY THE LORD DIRECT YOUR HEARTS INTO THE LOVE OF GOD AND INTO THE PATIENCE OF CHRIST." (2 Thes. 3:1-5)

12. Prayer for impartation of Holy Spirit boldness through the release of signs and wonders.

"...they raised their voice to God with one accord and said: 'Lord, You are God, who made heaven and earth and the sea... The kings of the earth took their stand, and the rulers were gathered together against the Lord and against His Christ. For truly against Your holy Servant Jesus, whom You anointed, both Herod and Pontius Pilate, with the Gentiles and the people of Israel, were gathered together to do whatever Your hand and Your purpose determined before to be done. Now, Lord, look on their threats, and GRANT TO YOUR SERVANTS THAT WITH ALL BOLDNESS THEY MAY SPEAK YOUR WORD, BY STRETCHING OUT YOUR HAND TO HEAL, AND THAT SIGNS AND WONDERS MAY BE DONE through the name of Your holy Servant Jesus.' And when they had prayed, the place where they were assembled together was shaken; and they were all filled with the Holy Spirit, and they spoke the word of God with boldness." (Acts 4:24-31)

Worship with the Word

What is worship? Worship is an expression of agreement with who God is. Worship is expressed in part by declaring the truth of who God is. We agree that He is who He says He is. For example, we say, "God, You are worthy. You are good."

What is "worship with the word? Worship with the word is a prayer format in which we agree with God's heart as we sing the biblical truths of who God is and what he promises to do.

Worship with the Word can help us to gain deeper revelation, knowledge and understanding about a specific Biblical passage or theme of Scripture. The worship team will focus on one specific passage or theme by singing through key verses from that passage or about that theme, using cross references and Biblical language. Doing this causes the Word to come alive to us.

The purpose of worship with the word is that we would encounter the living word, Jesus Christ, as we sing through, meditate on and study the written word.

Worship with the Word can be thought of as a "Singing Seminary." We grow in true revelation and intimacy with Jesus as we lovingly sing His Word back to His heart. We want to grow deeper and deeper in our understanding of God as revealed through Scripture and we want to develop an ability to express this revelation. We want to feel the Word burning in our hearts.

What Do I Do During a "Worship with the Word" Set

First, open your bible to the selected passage and ask the Holy Spirit to give you revelation of his word. At transition time, the prayer leader will announce to the room what passage of

Scripture the worship team will sing through for that set. There are a number of different things that you can do to engage with the Lord during a worship with the Word set: Ask God about it. Have a conversation with Him about His Word. It is very helpful to make a list of questions about the passage or verse(s). Even if you don't have questions about it, try and develop as many as you can. Ask all the inductive questions (who, what, when, where, why and how). Let Him speak to your heart. Just spend some time quieting your mind and directing your heart in love toward Him. Listen. Write down any revelation or thoughts.

Declare it. Take one verse or key idea from the passage and just say it quietly to yourself over and over. By declaring it, you are proclaiming that you believe it is true. It is amazing what can happen to our heart and mind when we simply declare truth over ourselves. Stir up your soul to believe the truth of what you are declaring.

Sing it. Just simply sing a verse or a couple of verses. We begin to feel more closely connected with the Word when we create and sing songs about it. Follow along with what the team is singing and/or make up your own antiphonal (responsive) phrases and choruses. Sing with your understanding and sing in the spirit as well.

Find cross-references. Look for other Bible verses that are similar to or expound on the verse that you are focusing on. The easiest way to do this is to use a concordance, which is usually found in the back section of most Bibles. You can also just try and use your own memory to think of other verses that are similar to the one you are looking at. Or, just start reading the Word and you will probably find something that will tie into the passage. You will find that cross-referencing will take you on a never-ending tour through the Word. Journal your thoughts about the verses and themes that you find.

Study it/read about it. Commentaries are an excellent way to get insight and understanding about the Word. You can get commentaries at the bookstore, the public library, or online.

Write about it.
1. Simply write your own explanation or understanding of the passage or verse(s).
2. Put the passage into your own words.
3. Write out your dialogue with God about it.
4. Write a story, poem, song, etc. about it.
5. Compose a comparison between the passage or verse(s) and another passage of Scripture.

My House shall be Called the House of Prayer

For other Books by Brondon Mathis:
Go to www.Amazon.com to order

1. <u>**Upon This Rock I will Build My Church**</u>. *The end-time purpose of the church built upon the book of the Revelation*

2. <u>**My Home shall be called a House of Prayer.**</u> *Our Family vision for training our children in the way they should go.*

3. <u>**The Coming Forerunner Ministry Out of Africa**</u> - *Africa & African America's end-time calling leading God's house of prayer to reconciliation and fullness.*

4. <u>**My Money is Restored**</u> - *The story of Joseph and the principles for the preparing to Arise during the coming financial fallout*

Contact info:
Brondon Mathis
614 467-0165, office
816-654-2186, cell
yeshuamovement@gmail.com
www.yeshualifecenter.com
facebook/brondonmathis.com

54981361R00140

Made in the USA
Charleston, SC
16 April 2016